Precarious Security

Books by Maxwell D. Taylor

Precarious Security
Swords and Plowshares
Responsibility and Response
The Uncertain Trumpet

Precarious Security

by
MAXWELL D. TAYLOR
GENERAL, U.S. ARMY (ret.)

W · W · NORTON & COMPANY · INC · New York

Copyright © 1976 by W. W. Norton & Company, Inc. All rights reserved.
Published simultaneously in Canada by George J. McLeod Limited,
Toronto. Printed in the United States of America.

First Edition

Library of Congress Cataloging in Publication Data

Taylor, Maxwell Davenport, 1901–
  Precarious security.

  Includes index.
  1. United States—National security. 2. United
States—Military policy. 3. United States—Defenses.
I. Title.
UA23.T318   355.03′3073   76–5798
ISBN 0–393–05579–5

This book was designed by Paula Wiener.
Typefaces used are Avanta and Roma Bold.
Manufacturing was done by The Haddon Craftsmen, Inc.
  2 3 4 5 6 7 8 9 0

To my sons, Jack and Tom

Contents

Foreword

If asked my justification for writing this book, I would plead a long dedication to the cause of national security and my present conviction of its precariousness in the next decade and thereafter. Insofar as the nature of the short-term future can be foreseen, it portends a period of change in the threats to our multiplying valuables—those assets, interests, and sources of power essential to our security and well-being. While the possibility of war in its historic manifestations will remain, there will be other forms of conflict, many capable of leading to war, arising from demographic, economic, and social causes. Many new developments highly unfavorable to our security are already perceptible—the progressive decline in power of the United States and its principal allies, the economic ills of the industrialized world, the continued malevolence of the Soviet Union backed by a growing military strength, the disruption of the power balance in the Mediterranean–Middle East, and growing unrest and discontent in the underdeveloped world.

At home, there are counterparts to these foreign threats—a decline in national unity and a rise in factionalism, inadequate government with leaders of diminished prestige and authority, and self-destructive and decadent traits in our society giving evidence of loss of will and ability to overcome the obstacles and challenges to our policies and interests.

If this evaluation of the future is even approximately correct, there is ample cause for feeling apprehension and for voicing an appeal for heeding the authentic needs of security. Under the postulated conditions, we must recognize that our security has become more than a military responsibility and that, in its broadened scope, it demands the protection of our valuables wherever found from threats of whatever kind, using all applicable forms of national power.

My self-appointed task is to outline a national security policy that will identify the sources of power available to provide such security and propose ways for maximizing the effectiveness of this power and for minimizing the waste inherent in present procedures. A major proposal for this purpose is the creation of an executive mechanism for integrating the power contributions from many governmental sources through an expansion of the organization and membership of the present National Security Council.

I shall expect criticism of the proposed national security policy on various grounds, one being that I have oversimplified many problems and have often ignored many of the technical difficulties. The fact is that I have wished to write a book that would appeal to interested laymen and therefore have attempted to circumvent, as far as possible, unnecessary complexities that would arise from detailed treatment of budgets, weapons systems, military force structures, and governmental organization—involved matters that tend to obscure the central issues. For a similar reason, I have avoided precise numerical estimates of such things as budget costs, levels of forces and weapons, and manpower requirements, except when they have appeared necessary to illustrate the general dimensions of the subject under discussion.

Although convinced that a national security policy such as I advocate is worth a determined trial, I must confess to a lack of faith in the improvement of the governmental apparatus as a primary means in itself for guaranteeing our future security. In the last analysis, we will be just as secure as we deserve. To achieve security, are we ready to commit ourselves and our children to pay the price in terms of public service and reduced living standards? Are we sufficiently clear-sighted to perceive the essential identity of our security and our well-being—that, in effect, they are opposite sides of a single coin of great value? If so, we will understand that we cannot enjoy well-being if insecure or security if deprived of a quality of life worth defending.

But recognition of the essentiality of security and possession of a will to sacrifice for its achievement are still not enough. We must somehow learn to suppress the self-destructive and degenerate ways we have acquired of late—attitudes and practices that play into the hands of our enemies and contain the seeds of eventual disaster. The list is long and includes failings such as the habitual denigration of our leaders and institutions, self-defamation, self-intimidation, loss of faith in the American system, and a distorted view of life which limits our perception to the evil, duplicity, and corruption in the world around us. These are traits that in history have often preceded the decadence of a civilization and the appearance of predatory barbarians at its gates.

As in my past essays in authorship, I am deeply indebted to my wife, Diddy, who has overlooked the habitual untidiness of my study in the course of my literary activities while continuing to encourage me to pursue them. My son Jack and his wife Priscilla have been most helpful in reading, criticizing, and suggesting improvements in the manuscript. Their efforts have been reinforced by the experienced judgment of Evan Thomas, vice-president of W. W. Norton & Company, who has been my editorial advisor in this, our fourth literary venture together.

M.D.T.

Precarious Security

I

National Security in a Changing Environment

As we Americans contemplate the probable course of national and international affairs during the remainder of this century, it is easy to find causes for pessimism in the experiences of the recent past and to assume that current fears and misgivings will of necessity prolong themselves into the future. As I write in 1975, the economic outlook for the United States and the Western world offers a gloomy prospect of continued inflation and recession, an indefinite shortage of energy with prolonged vassalage to the oil producers of OPEC, a growing scarcity of food and raw materials, and a threat of new cartels on the oil model. The Arab-Israeli conflict seems incapable of solution, carrying with it the ever-present possibility of a military collision with the Soviet Union. There is always a vague fear of nuclear war, presently reinforced by the danger of a further proliferation of nuclear weapons possibly in highly irresponsible hands.

Even the environment seems permeated by inimical forces producing overpopulation, famine, pollution, drought, and other natural disasters—conditions that are becoming global in extent and so vast as to defy the efforts of governments to cope with them. Our hopes in the United Nations as an agency of international cooperation capable of dealing with such matters have been largely dissipated by the evidence of demagoguery and factionalism in the General Assem-

1

bly. We perceive no supermen at home or abroad to lead us safely through this maze of snares and pitfalls.

Such conditions produce justified fears for the security of those things to which we attach great value both as individuals and as citizens of the nation. Many of these valuables are personal to us and our families—life, health, happiness, financial security. Others are national treasures which we share with our fellow citizens—the assets, interests, and aspirations of the entire nation. We look to our leaders to provide ample protection to valuables of both sorts, and in so doing we acknowledge the reality of national security as a prime purpose of government of immediate concern to all Americans. As we enter a period that appears rife with potential troubles, it is a fitting time to appraise the future tasks of protecting our valuables and determine the elements of an adequate and reasonable security policy under the conditions anticipated.

At the start of such an appraisal, there will be at least two obstacles to overcome: one, a prejudice; the other, a misunderstanding. As an aftereffect of the Vietnam war and the Watergate scandals, national security, once a slogan for rallying citizens to the ramparts of the Republic, has fallen into disrepute in many quarters and for some has become an object of derision. Like the military uniform, it has symbolized a highly unpopular war and has shared in its disfavor. In unsavory Watergate episodes, "national security" seemed often to be used as an excuse for illegal encroachments on civil liberties or as a cloak to conceal official blunders, misdoings, and even crimes. To paraphrase Samuel Johnson, national security appeared to have become the last refuge of scoundrels.

The second obstacle is to remove the vagueness that has surrounded the popular concept of national security even in its halcyon days. Even though it is a term we use without hesitation, and one that often appears in the laws of the land, I know of no official source that has ever undertaken its definition. The omission exists even in the National Security Act of 1947, which had the primary purpose of strengthening the institutions, organizations, and procedures related to it. In the absence of a clear definition, its nature remains shrouded today in ambiguity which is a continuing obstacle to understanding its scope and content.

Most Americans have been accustomed to regard national security as something having to do with the military defense of the country against a military enemy, and thus as a responsibility primarily of the armed forces. We appear to have retained the view of the founding fathers that the "common defense" needs only a "well-regulated militia" ready to suppress insurrections or repel invasions. Admiral Mahan, writing at the turn of the twentieth century, expressed a somewhat similar feeling that the needs of our security "can best be met by a navy at sea far from the national territory."

Experience in defending our interests in the course of this century should have modified this narrow traditional view. Particularly in World War II and the ensuing cold war, we have had ample evidence of the harm that can be done by nonmilitary means employed by unfriendly governments—diplomatic machinations, economic and psychological warfare, political subversion, defamatory propaganda, terrorism, and paramilitary violence. While such weapons have been used repeatedly against us, we have failed to take seriously the essentiality of designing countermeasures to cope with them in the future.

To remove past ambiguities and recognize the widened spectrum of threats to our security, we should recognize that adequate protection in the future must embrace all important valuables, tangible or otherwise, in the form of assets, national interests, or sources of future strength. Tangible assets include such things as our constitutional form of government and the institutions devolving from it; the wealth and natural resources of our homeland; our overseas possessions and investments; the armed forces and their bases abroad. Assets may also be intangible or spiritual—freedom, national unity, reputation, and self-confidence.

The term *national interest,* used to describe a class of valuables, requires clarification. In this discussion, it will refer to anything of value that the President and Congress regard as so essential for the nation to gain, retain, or enjoy as to be deemed worthy of the expenditure of significant national resources. In practice, a national interest is often a broad objective of foreign or domestic policy expressed in such general terms as a peaceful environment, the nonproliferation of nuclear weapons, a stable economy, or quality education in our schools. Other times, the language may be more specific—self-determination for South Vietnam, independence from foreign oil by 1985, or the removal of Soviet missiles from Cuba. The test of a bona fide national interest is the willingness of the country to expend resources for its attainment—otherwise it is merely a pious principle or benevolent intention.

Sources of strength may be found in the quality of our leaders and people, in the productivity of the economy, in the strength we draw from alliances, and in the character-formative forces that shape the mind and behavior of new generations—in times past, the task of the home, school, church, and national culture.

An adequate national security policy must provide ample protection for the foregoing classes of valuables, wherever found, from dangers military and nonmilitary, foreign and domestic, utilizing for the purpose all appropriate forms of national power.

Taking this broadened concept of national security as a point of departure, we shall try to identify the components of a national security policy that will provide the protection implicit in the concept and that, at the same time, will be sufficiently rational and reasonable to attract the popular support essential for its success. Such a policy must of necessity take into account the trends and conditions to be anticipated in the future environment that may affect the security of the valuables which are the object of our concern.

With the task thus defined, the first item of business becomes an identification of the elements of the emerging international and domestic scene that bear upon the purposes, ways, and means of national security—in short, a venturesome excursion into the risky business of forecasting the future. Past experience in long-range military planning has demonstrated to my satisfaction that any such exercise, despite its purported long range, turns out to be little more than a projection into the future of present conditions with minor modifications. There is always an inability in the seer community to anticipate the emergence of some unheralded world leader, the unexpected explosion of some smoldering political or social volcano, or a technological discovery that will open up a completely new field of scientific achievement.

Another professional disability of prophets, reaching back to Biblical times, is their tendency to foresee only evil and disaster, never the more pleasant possibilities of the future. Like modern media, they apparently believe that only bad news is newsworthy, or that since happy events call for no preventive action they require no prophetic warning. But whatever their motivation, history shows that bearers of ill tidings run considerable risks—in fact, they may even lose their heads. At the moment this is an unhappy thought since any conscientious appraisal of the future environment must include a depressingly long list of possible dangers, troublemakers, and malevolent forces.

There is today at least one reliable clue to assist in a forecast of the coming period—the existence of population growth as a constant factor of increasing but predictable dimensions. By modern demographic methods, the growth of national populations can be estimated with fair accuracy to the end of the century, even though, in the meantime, governments may do their best to reduce the national growth rate. According to such calculations, by the year 2000 the world population will at least double with the greatest densities concentrated in countries least prepared to support them— South Asia, China, Indonesia, Africa, the Middle East, and tropical Latin America.

By the end of the century, in South Asia, where starvation is frequent today in a population of 770 million, there will be about 1.4 billion people struggling for survival. China, which currently must often import large quantities of grain to feed 820 million, must find food for more than a billion to escape mass starvation. Indonesia, faced with the problem of accommodating over 230 million by the year 2000, will envy the vast open spaces of neighboring Australia, which by that time will be sustaining only about 20 million. Brazil, with over 200 million at the end of the century, will tower over its neighbors Argentina, Chile, and Uruguay, whose combined populations total only about a fourth of Brazil's. Some 3 million Israelis are today encircled by 70 million hostile Arab neighbors who will double in number by the year 2000, while Israel adds perhaps 2 million. Mexican "wetbacks" now pour illegally into our southwestern states at an annual rate believed to be over 800,000. What will be the extent of the invasion at the end of the century when the population of Mexico will have nearly doubled or by 2025 when it may approximate that of the United States?

Such considerations justify a conviction that population growth and population-related problems will be a dominant, pernicious factor in the future development of nations and their relations with one another. The consequences will endanger not just American security but that of the world community.

One such consequence, of which we can be as sure as we are of population growth itself, is a continuing food shortage, which has already reached famine proportions in many densely populated countries. With the United States and Canada the only countries likely to have surplus food in quantity for export in the years ahead, we may expect an enormous demand for our agricultural products far exceeding availability. While our food exports will constitute an asset of great political and economic value, we shall also have a heavy responsibility in determining its use, a decision that will involve the lives of millions. This question is likely to become a divisive national issue and, whatever our policy, it will create enmity for us in many parts of an insatiably hungry world.

Another characteristic of the period which seems reasonably certain is a widespread popular discontent with governments that fail to cope with the complex problems that will face them. There will be no easy solution to expanding populations, declining natural resources, chronic inflation, recurrent cycles of industrial recession, and growing pollution and depletion of the environment. Leaders of Western democracies unable or afraid to ask the necessary sacrifices of their electorates in time to prevent disaster will be vulnerable to sudden voter rejection in expiation of their failure to perform miracles.

Against this background of relatively certain developments, we may identify other problem areas that, without having the same degree of inevitability, still merit serious consideration in our planning. It seems reasonable to believe that great power relationships will retain the current pentagonal pattern linking the United States, the USSR, Western Europe, Japan, and the People's Republic of China (PRC). The present members of this club display all or some of the attributes normally associated with great power status: stable government; a numerous, gifted people; wealth derived from economic productivity; substantial armed forces; and a past record of star performance on the world stage. The United States and USSR come nearest to qualifying on all counts, whereas all the others have certain shortcomings—Western Europe suffers from economic and political weaknesses; Japan from a shortage of natural resources and effective armed forces; and China from serious internal problems arising from uncertainty as to the devolution of power after Mao. Despite defects of some of the members, the pentagonal club consists of power centers each capable of playing an important role in future world affairs.

The stability of relationships among these powers will be of great importance since heads of state will always be concerned lest some shift change the existing equilibrium to their disadvantage. The United States will be particularly watchful of Soviet-PRC conduct since any rapprochement between the two would raise the specter of a revived Sino-Soviet bloc menacing the non-Communist world. Similarly, we will be wary of important economic understandings between the USSR and Japan, an arrangement that might appeal to the Japanese as a means for assuring sources of energy and raw materials to support a resource-poor economy.

We shall feel anxiety over the continued vitality of Western Europe because of the internal weakness displayed by most of our allies in that region. European reactions to the Middle East war, to the oil embargo, and to the Cyprus crisis have revealed the fragility of the NATO alliance and its negligible value to us in dealing with political or economic problems outside the NATO area. Europeans in turn are uneasy over our highly advertised détente with the USSR, which to them is a warning that the Americans may not feel as strongly as formerly that their security is inextricably linked to that of Europe.

Although Japan has shown surprising resilience under the pressures of inflation and exorbitant oil prices, it remains a truncated power without vital natural resources under its own control and without the military strength to defend its immediate interests. However, the United States will continue to view relations with Japan as the key to our Asian policy, just as NATO has been the cornerstone of our foreign policy on the other side of the globe. Nevertheless, this relationship is likely to continue to be an uncomfortable one for both parties—the Japanese unsure of our reliability as a military protector and trade partner, the United States frustrated by the difficulty of understanding an enigmatic and painfully sensitive ally still smarting from brusque treatment accorded by the Nixon administration. If we really expect the Japanese to share our burdens in maintaining peace and stability in the Western Pacific, it will be in our interest for Japan to assure the sources of raw materials essential for its survival as an economic power and its continuance as a market for American exports.

We can hardly forecast future relations with China until we know the new leadership that will replace Mao and Chou En-lai. The internal problems resulting from excessive population and food shortages, the continued military threat of the USSR on its western frontiers, and the strains and tensions inherent in a change in leadership will make it unlikely that the PRC will play a dynamic international role in the relatively short period surveyed here.

From the American viewpoint, the key figure in the pentagonal club is likely to remain the USSR. If one had a reliable blueprint of future Soviet behavior, it would not be difficult to chart a sound course for American foreign policy with some confidence. Unfortunately, the indicators of future Soviet behavior are few in number, blurred at best, and often mutually contradictory. While apparently committed to *détente* as long as it brings access to United States capital and technology, the Soviets are expending vast resources to increase their strategic and conventional armaments while expanding their fleet to assume a global maritime role. During periods of tension in the Middle East, they have been intermittent troublemakers, often egging on Arab oil producers to squeeze ever-higher prices from Western consumers. As viewed happily from Moscow, the oil crisis is in effect a form of economic warfare waged by Arab proxies that undermines the capitalist system and thus serves the ultimate purpose of communism.

For the short term, it appears likely that the Soviets will continue to avoid direct military confrontation with the United States, while indulging in their favorite pastime of fishing in troubled waters and confidently awaiting the downfall of capitalism from its internal weaknesses—sometimes giving a helping hand to the inevitable.

As already forecast, economic factors are likely to play a greater role than ever before in determining the behavior of nations. Oil, food, and fertilizer are already scarce in many places or available only at extremely high prices. Observing the dramatic success of the oil cartel, producers of bauxite, copper, phosphate, iron, and manganese are increasing their efforts to obtain a greater return from their products. Exporters of tin, rubber, and chrome are being encouraged to join in the price-jacking game. There is a movement among Latin American nations to form a regional group to control much of the trade with the United States in order to obtain better terms for their exports and imports. The cartel weapon seems sure to enjoy increasing popularity.

Meanwhile, American demand for imports of oil and minerals is constantly increasing, although our dependence on foreign sources is still slight in comparison to that of Europe and Japan. However, our payments for Middle East oil are already a painful burden and we can expect eventually a somewhat similar situation in the case of many minerals. A 1974 government estimate forecasts a $60-billion increase in United States expenditures for minerals in the next twenty-five years.

World-wide shortages of fuel and raw materials will progressively generate intense international competition in exploring and exploiting new sources. Coastal waters and particularly the rich sea bed will become zones of contention where nations will stake out and defend their claims by persuasion, appeals to international opinion, litigation, or even force of arms. Naval powers will use their fleets to maintain maritime communications with external sources of materials and to defend the installations and pipelines related to extractive operations on the sea floor. This era of shortages and high prices of raw materials will be particularly difficult for the industrial powers, already suffering from inflation, recession, and unemployment, and living under a threat of a declining standard of living, highly disturbing to elected officials.

This may be a suitable place to comment on the multiple impact of the OPEC action in quadrupling the world price of oil. The consequences have been not merely economic but political and military as well. The high prices have caused the movement of billions of dollars to the oil producers at such a rate as to preclude the formulation of an orderly long-term investment policy for the use of their newly acquired wealth. Such investments or deposits as they have made in the West have thus far been generally short-term—an arrangement that offers them an opportunity to do serious mischief through sudden withdrawals of funds from foreign accounts. While national oil bills in 1975 have been met, it is far from clear how long weak industrial countries like Italy can continue to do so whereas many developing countries with little to sell abroad will soon reach the end of their rope and will require help to survive. In the United States, our rising expenditures for foreign oil, although still relatively modest, have contributed to inflated commodity prices, trade deficits, and the forces of recession. Still without a long-term energy policy, we must anticipate growing dependence on Mideast oil, reaching by 1977 about 80 per cent of our oil imports. At this rate our vulnerability to OPEC pressures will soon approximate that of Europe and Japan.

The oil weapon inspires such fear in Western Europe that our allies have been deterred from playing a constructive role in maintaining peace in the Middle East despite their vital interest in its stability.

Fearful of a new oil embargo, in 1973 they opposed the movement of American equipment from the NATO area to replace Israeli losses in the Autumn War. This fear of the oil weapon is capable of nullifying the military potential of an alliance that cannot fight for long without oil. Even if the producers were willing to supply oil, dependence on Mideast sources poses a serious problem to NATO naval forces which, in a confrontation with the Warsaw Pact, must assure tanker routes from the Persian Gulf to European ports, mostly around Africa. While the OPEC hold on the United States is not yet so firm, even now Washington must think twice before taking any action that might renew the oil embargo.

This ability of the oil producers to use their monopoly to blackmail consumers and influence their foreign policy constitutes an added threat to the security of Israel, dependent as it is on aid from the United States. The threat became more direct when Arab states began to buy large supplies of the most modern conventional weapons from Western markets, including the United States. They would also have ample funds to hire Western technicians, pilots, and even mercenary combat units—possibly a modern version of the Turkish Janizaries of old—if their leaders felt the need. Their wealth could also buy the means to produce nuclear weapons or the weapons themselves, if a venal seller could be found.

Thus the use which the oil-rich nations make of their great wealth will be an important force in shaping events in the next decade. The wisdom or folly they display is likely to determine the political and economic destiny of a large part of the world and influence the choice of war or reason as a solution of the contentious issues that will arise. Let us hope that OPEC will not overplay its hand and provoke reprisals by Western nations menaced with the "strangulation," which Secretary Kissinger has mentioned as a possible justification for a consumer resort to arms.

Recognition of the power of the oil cartel for good or evil raises the question of the proper place of this coalition in the world power structure. Are these oil-producing countries in the aggregate on a par with Western Europe or Japan and entitled to a sixth seat in the pentagonal club? Or is OPEC a transitory power center that will dissipate with the development of petroleum substitutes in the West or with the gradual exhaustion of their oil reserves?

If we apply the criteria of great power status previously discussed, the Arab countries of OPEC, generally speaking, do not enjoy the advantages of stable government, of large, talented populations, or of a record of significant historical achievement in recent centuries. For generations they have been miserably poor, backward, militarily impotent, and politically disunited. Now oil has suddenly made many rich; a common hatred of Israel has given them a unifying purpose; and demonstrated ability to intimidate Western nations has stimulated a thirst for further power. But sudden wealth has not provided them with wise and able leadership, ended their backwardness, or eliminated the root causes of Arab disunity. Hence, on present evidence, I would say that this potent cartel has not yet earned great power status but for the moment at least, commands the deference of all industrial powers and the obeisance of those developing countries dependent on Arab largess for survival.

The have-not segment of the international community is the most difficult to appraise in terms of future influence on world conditions. These nations represent three fourths of the world population and include large countries with ancient cultures and proud histories like China and India as well as miniscule tribal states devoid of leadership, political experience, or a sense of nationhood. While their conditions differ widely, most of them are burdened with problems beyond their own ability to resolve.

Many of their troubles are the consequences of overpopulation. Their economic difficulties are often aggravated by the poor quality or shortage of natural resources, by dependence on one major crop such as coffee or sugar in Latin America, and more recently by the high cost of imported manufactures and petroleum products. Usually lacking capital, managerial experience, and skilled labor, they have little chance to develop an indigenous industry, or even one capable of meeting their own immediate needs. Their most urgent problem in most cases is food, already increasingly in world-wide short supply and certain to become more so. The number of mouths to feed in the world continues to grow, readily available agricultural land is overworked, irrigation is often inadequate, and chemical fertilizers are both scarce and costly. Starvation areas are appearing in many places in Asia and Africa, often accompanied by drought or flood resulting from environmental impairment.

Such desperate conditions among the have-nots will have reasonably predictable effects. Many local governments, unable to cope with such problems, will collapse or be overturned by popular discontent. Democratic regimes, fragile at best in the Third World, are likely to be replaced by dictatorships, often under military leadership. Resentment will mount against the have-powers, particularly against the notoriously affluent and wasteful United States, which will be held responsible for the high prices of food and industrial imports. In central and southern Africa, resentment may take the form of black versus white; in Southeast Asia, brown Asians versus white Australians and New Zealanders; in the Western Hemisphere, Latins versus Yanquis. Efforts on the part of the have-nots will increase to unite against the haves and to use the United Nations as an instrument for their purposes.

In summary, during the next decade one may anticipate that many underdeveloped nations will be the scene of natural disasters, changes in government, conflicts with neighbors over living space and resources, and hostile reactions against real and imaginary external enemies held responsible for their plight. Environmental conditions may be conducive to renewed outbreaks of old animosities—Jew versus Arab, Hindu versus Moslem or Chinese. They may revive hostilities in divided countries—Korea and Vietnam, for example—or between rival ideologies—the Soviet version of communism against the Chinese brand. The prospect is one of a decade replete with conflicts contributing to political instability, social turbulence, civil and foreign wars.

The Indian nuclear test in late 1974 was a reminder that further proliferation of nuclear weapons will be a likely development in this period. More countries will acquire some or all of the ingredients necessary for making their own weapons—money, advanced technology, engineering, and industrial know-how along with the required raw materials. Failing any of these assets, a country aspiring to the nuclear club may obtain help from external sources or may even buy finished weapons, as I have suggested in the case of the OPEC countries.

Why should a country wish to acquire nuclear weapons? There are two probable motives: fear of aggression by a superior enemy and/or desire for prestige with the attendant political leverage. If one searches the world atlas for countries likely to be so motivated, it is possible to identify several with reason to fear aggression which they could probably not resist by present means: Israel, menaced by growing Arab strength; Egypt and Syria, fearing another surprise attack by Israel; Iraq, suspicious of Iran; Iran, on guard to the north because of the aggressive record of the USSR; Pakistan, ever-mindful of the traditional hostility of India; India, remembering the Chinese attack in 1962; South Korea, in constant alarm over North Korea; South Africa–Rhodesia, beleaguered by hostile black neighbors; Australia, sensing the envy of its open spaces by neighboring Asian masses; Argentina, overshadowed by the growing size and strength of Brazil.

Desire for prestige might incite virtually any country to "go nuclear," with the possibility particularly strong in the case of India, Iran, Libya, Brazil, and Venezuela. West Germany and Japan might be suspected of motivation from both sources; however, the acquisition of nuclear weapons by either would have such adverse effects on the foreign relations of both countries as to make such action unlikely at least in the near future.

In the meantime, the expansion of the nuclear club moves forward slowly without any serious effort in the international community to arrest it. India exploded its "peaceful device" and received only mild reproaches in rebuke. Israel is generally credited with already having "nuclear devices," which it may unveil with maximum effect at some critical point in its relations with the Arabs.

The consequences of continued proliferation are difficult to quantify but are sure to present responsible world leaders with difficult dilemmas. If proliferation is not arrested, the presence of nuclear weapons in additional countries may cause the United States and the USSR to reconsider the need for antiballistic missile and bomber defenses for their homelands and possibly to add an additional incre- ment to the nuclear stockpile to provide weapons for use against gate-crashers of the nuclear club. Another danger from proliferation will be the increased possibility of nuclear accidents, human mistakes, weapon seizures by terrorists, and more proliferation to keep up with the neighbors.

Is military action to prevent proliferation unthinkable? Possibly not, particularly if a country bent on prevention had accurate long- range conventional weapons to do the job. If nuclear weapons fell into the hands of unbalanced leaders, international action to evict them forcibly from power would be as justifiable a defensive measure as a pre-emptive attack to destroy the weapons themselves.

In such an environment what will be the probability of overt warfare between nations? It seems reasonable to assume that a fear of consequences added to a rational interpretation of self-interest will continue to restrain a deliberate resort to strategic nuclear weapons by the present nuclear powers. Large-scale conventional wars with or without the use of battlefield nuclear weapons are within the capabil- ity only of industrial powers with war-sustaining economies. How- ever, as we have noted, many such countries in the West suffer from weak governments enjoying limited popular support and having elec- torates with little enthusiasm for military ventures. Hence, without ruling out the possibility, one is inclined to give the big war threat a low probability rating insofar as the Western democracies and Japan are concerned. The USSR also is likely to wish to avoid major war, but for different reasons—the restraining fear of inducing seri- ous trouble with China and the hope that economic forces will of themselves do in the rival capitalist world.

On the other hand, in the turbulent, volatile environment that we are postulating, the probability of minor military conflicts is very high. American leaders will be called upon to face many crises, often unpredictable, which may require the threat or use of armed force to control them. They may be obliged to make decisions on the use of military force to rescue Israel from disaster, to prevent stragulation by the OPEC cartel, to restore order or to protect American nationals in some chaotic emerging state, to repel predators threatening American interests offshore or on the ocean floor, or to respond to a request for help from some ally. Or there may be the question of how to react to a military conflict breaking out along some politically sensitive frontier—for example, the border between East and West Germany, North and South Korea, or China and the USSR. Such possibilities exist today, and the future will undoubtedly generate others of equal or greater urgency which cannot be foreseen.

If one accepts all or most of this estimate of the future environment, there are ample grounds to support a number of conclusions regarding the likely impact on our national security. In the great power community, the USSR will remain the cynosure of our political and military attention. While strategic nuclear war can probably be deterred and major war involving important industrial nations seems relatively unlikely, there is a high probability of innumerable frictions and collisions of national interests capable of creating dangerous international tensions leading to a resort to military force.

The predominant nonmilitary threats to our security in this period will be economic, at least in their initial form, and will require extensive nonmilitary means to forestall or neutralize them if military action is to be avoided.

Population growth and shortages of food, fertilizer, energy and minerals will create serious problems in industrial countries and disasters in much of the developing world.

The United States will need the help of allies and of responsible governments of all descriptions to improve the lot of the have-nots and to cope with the many global problems transcending national capabilities. For maximum effectiveness in using our own resources, we must learn to utilize all forms of power in support of national policy in this turbulent period.

II

Policy Goals and National Security

A constant problem of government is to prevent the goals of national policy from outrunning the means necessary for their achievement and the subsequent requirements for protection of the assets thus acquired. If we are to design an adequate national security policy we must give thought to some of the policies that our leaders may wish to pursue and appraise the demands that such policies may place on the resources of national security.

Over the years a major problem for security planners has been to obtain official guidance as to the likely goals of national policy expressed in sufficiently precise terms to be of practical help in determining future security needs. For various reasons, such guidance has rarely been available at the proper time. For one thing, busy senior officials capable of providing it are usually so engrossed in day-to-day tasks that they have little leisure for serious thought about a future beyond the next federal budget. Also, it is a risky business for a senior politician to put on public record an estimate of future events which, if wide of the mark, would provide ammunition to his adversaries. Similarly, a president who announces specific policy goals affords the public a measure of his failure if he falls short of his hopes. Hence it is common practice for officials to define foreign policy goals in the broad generalities of peace, prosperity, cooperation, and good will—

unimpeachable as ideals but of little use in determining the specific objectives we are likely to pursue, and the time, place, and intensity of our efforts.

For the purposes of this study, we are in the same boat as the unguided security planner in government—we must form our own judgment first as to the future environment as we have already done and then as to the objectives that our leaders are likely to choose and the impact of these choices on national security.

In the field of foreign policy, for reasons previously mentioned, our leaders will be obliged to pay close attention to great power relations in order to assure a continuing favorable balance of power. In particular, we shall want a close relationship with Western Europe and Japan while keeping a close eye on the USSR. We should like to keep the Soviets isolated in the pentagonal power club with no surreptitious liaisons developing either with Japan or China. We shall want to probe the sincerity of their commitment to *détente* and to arms limitation and, if possible, explore the feasibility of obtaining their cooperation in reaching a long-term settlement in the Mideast. Impressed with the international dangers arising from nuclear proliferation, we might try to enlist Soviet assistance in resisting this trend, or at least in discouraging further nations from "going nuclear." Meantime, we would like to understand the purpose of their naval expansion and their seeming willingness to expend unlimited resources needlessly on additional strategic weapons.

It may justify a digression at this point to wonder whether the quest of a *détente* will remain a fixture of Soviet-American policy in the period in which we are interested. On the assumption that it describes a relationship between the two countries characterized by honest efforts to dampen mutual hostility, fear, or suspicion, its pursuit as a long-term policy objective would seem clearly in the best interest of both powers, provided that improved relations were accompanied by clear evidence of consistently cooperative behavior by both sides.

Thus far, although *détente* can claim some success, such evidence is not available. In its name, Washington and Moscow have opened channels of communication between their heads of state and have increased personal contacts among senior officials. The Soviets continue to emit anti-American propaganda but in moderated volume and tone. Manners in formal discussions have improved to the point that no Moscow representative has found it necessary of late to emphasize a point by table thumping with his shoe. While the SALT talks on the limitation of strategic arms have been painfully slow, Communist negotiators are never in a hurry, and eventually some concessions have been made by both sides. Also, both parties have shown intermittent interest in widening trade relations.

Détente has also known some flagrant failures. Under their interpretation of its meaning, the Soviets have not felt restrained from interposing obstacles to Dr. Kissinger's mediation in the Arab-Israeli quarrel or from urging OPEC to increase the price of oil charged their Western customers. Until the final collapse of the South Vietnamese forces in 1975, the Soviets never ceased to supply Hanoi with weapons to continue the aggression against the South in violation of the 1973 cease-fire. As a major cause for concern, the vast Soviet expenditures on armaments display a continued determination to surpass the United States as a military power and the hope eventually to take undisputed first place in the rank of great powers.

No doubt Moscow has similar complaints to level at the United States. It could point to the Senate action conditioning a U.S. grant of most-favored-nation status in trade relations to the USSR upon increased freedom for Jews to emigrate from Russia. The Soviets would probably also complain that Kissinger had maneuvered to exclude them from any significant role in a Mideast settlement.

In short, *détente* as an effort to improve United States–Soviet relations has had its ups and downs and probably will never be entirely satisfactory to either party. However, the mutual need to live together without a major collision is so obvious that attempts at *détente,* perhaps under a different name, seem likely to continue more or less indefinitely. But in the meantime, each side will wish to prevent any significant accretion in power by the other while keeping a watchful, skeptical eye on all activities of the rival. In all the bargaining that will take place, I would expect the Soviets to give as little as possible while getting the maximum possible, patiently awaiting the Marxist day of judgment when the walls of capitalism will come tumbling down.

Throughout history, the Mideast has been an international crossroads where the interests of many nations intersect. It remains so today and promises to grow in importance with the increasing economic and military power of Iran and the oil-rich Arab states. But it is difficult to foresee the precise direction of American policy in the area until a final settlement of the Arab-Israeli conflict, which presently keeps regional relations in a dangerous turmoil.

We can only hope that wise policy makers will steer a safe course through the treacherous currents of Mideast politics. They must not lose sight of the hard realities of future power relations in this area, where the Arabs will grow steadily in population, wealth, and armaments while Israel remains stunted in growth and devoid of powerful friends save the United States. Under such conditions, which seem unlikely to change, the long-term survival of Israel will depend on its winning somehow the ungrudging acceptance of its existence by its Arab neighbors, accompanied by some kind of international guarantee of a terminal settlement that will include the United States and the USSR. Israel cannot live indefinitely as a beleaguered, resource-poor enclave surrounded by aggressively hostile neighbors, no matter what the United States is willing to provide.

Outside the Mideast, policy objectives vis-à-vis the developing world are difficult to anticipate in specific form because of the wide differences among the countries of the so-called Third World. Nations like India, Honduras, and Chad have little in common except excessive population, abject human misery, and a tropical climate. While we may adopt the general goal of improving the lot of the hungry and disadvantaged of the world to the best of our ability, it will not be easy to decide how to distribute our limited resources.

Faced with conditions of poverty and backwardness affecting most of the world population, our leaders must surely seek help and cooperation from other have-nations and from international organizations, particularly the United Nations. They must try to persuade countries like Saudi Arabia, Iran, Nigeria, and Venezuela to do their fair share in helping have-not neighbors in distress. This need for help from foreign sources should provide an incentive for re-examining our formal alliances to see whether they are relevant to changing conditions.

In the binge of alliance—making following World War II, our prime purpose was to obtain military cooperation in resisting further Communist aggression and territorial expansion. This was a justified concern at the time; but in an era of economic scarcities, cartel price jacking, competition for new resources, and resort to various forms of economic warfare, our need for help from foreign nations is changing. Henceforth, we shall be interested in obtaining formal understandings with principal trade partners and exporters of scarce raw materials to assure continued satisfaction of our growing industrial needs. Military contributions by allies are likely to assume a secondary importance. Thus a policy objective in this period should be an updating and revitalizing of alliances with economic factors receiving their belated due in the light of newly perceived dangers.

Thus far we have considered a few of the probable goals of foreign policy most likely to have a significant impact on national security. Are there goals of domestic policy also in this category? While in the past we have ordinarily felt that national security was a concern largely of foreign policy and national well-being the substance of domestic policy, under the broadened concept of security herein advocated that distinction no longer holds. Many of the valuables requiring the protection of national security—peace, national unity, free trade, political and economic stability—are of vital concern to domestic policy, whereas both foreign and domestic policy draw their support from a single national pool of human and material resources. Thus, domestic policy influences and is influenced by national security—a reason to inquire into the goals of domestic policy which may impinge upon it.

The overall goal of domestic policy in a democracy is normally simple and constant—an electorate sufficiently satisfied with the current government to leave it indefinitely in power. But to achieve this ideal is a complicated and exacting problem, a source of constant anguish to officeholders. While politicians now as in the past will try to avoid actions causing unhappiness to their constituents, they will have great difficulty in resolving many of the problems that we have foreseen without damage either to the comfort or to the life style of the voter.

We already feel the weight of the tax burden developing from the social benefits afforded our citizens, a burden that will increase rapidly in the coming years. To moderate the pain of paying this social bill, there will be increasing pressure on Congress to reduce expenditures in the foreign and military fields. This trend may reverse direction suddenly for a short while, but the competition between foreign and domestic programs is likely to be a persistent phenomenon with popular sentiment usually on the side of more social security at the price of less national security.

Our domestic policy of achieving independence from OPEC is motivated to a large extent by considerations of national security, yet it may produce side effects adverse thereto. Its implementation may incite reprisals from the oil cartelists in the form of new increases in the price of oil or financial manipulations prejudicial to our economic stability. If pursuit of the energy policy results in domestic hardships, that fact will turn the electorate against the responsible officials and add to the discontent with government.

There are numerous other domestic policies that may have repercussions on national security—for example, the policy to be pursued in exporting our food surpluses in a period when starvation will be threatening large masses of the world population. How much will we be willing to reduce American consumption to provide more exports for the hungry abroad? Should the government use our food surpluses for political, economic, or humanitarian purposes or for some combination? To whom will we sell or give our food with so many claimants appealing for help? However our policy makers decide such questions, they will be condemned both at home and abroad, though frequently for contrary reasons. In the end, domestic food policy may contribute more to discord than to peace, more to promote anti-American feeling among the hungry than their gratitude for the life-sustaining contributions of the American farmer.

As we become more impressed with the dangers of population growth and devote more effort to the control of our national birthrate, it is probable that immigration policy will regain some of the political importance it had before World War II, when the American West Coast lived in fear of an Oriental immigrant invasion. In 1975 we are admitting about 400,000 legal immigrants, while at least twice that number will enter illegally. As population pressures rise abroad, particularly in Mexico and the Caribbean countries, this influx, legal and illegal, will surely increase and raise a public cry for strong anti-immigration legislation. As in the case of food, this issue could augment internal dissension and arouse new have-not animosities against us, particularly in Latin American countries which contain many of the raw materials that our industry must import in the future.

The interplay of partisan domestic politics may occasionally produce effects adverse to the purposes of national security. It is not uncommon for political leaders to take positions on foreign issues with an eye more on ethnic voter reactions than on the national interest. The action of Congress in 1975 in interrupting military aid to Turkey in response to Greek minority pressure deeply offended our most important ally in the Mediterranean, compromised our base rights there, and seriously impaired the effectiveness of American diplomats engaged in seeking a Cyprus settlement. Because of apartheid in South Africa and Rhodesia, American blacks and antisegregation groups have pressured Congress for sanctions against the all-white regimes. Unfortunately, these countries are important to us because of their mineral exports and their strategic position in relation to the maritime routes around Africa.

Since Americans in general have an instinctive dislike for governments controlled by dictatorships and military juntas, particularly those of the right, many politicians view them as fair targets for threatening gesticulation. While they have usually limited the expression of their displeasure to vocal criticism and threats, they have sometimes taken actions seriously complicating our relations with countries like Greece, Spain, South Korea, Chile, and South Vietnam. In the latter case, anti-Thieu bias was a definite factor in the interruption of American aid after the 1973 cease-fire which contributed heavily to the ultimate debacle.

By and large, the record shows that such interventions in foreign policy inspired more by domestic politics than by broad national considerations have produced far more harm than good. Sometimes, they have raised resentment against the United States in countries whose cooperation we have needed; sometimes, as in the issue of Jewish emigration from Russia, congressional intervention has worked against its intended purpose and, in this case, has produced a reduction in the number of Jewish emigrants. In virtually all cases we have paid some price in domestic acrimony generated among ourselves. The negative results support the conclusion that the cause of political idealism would be better served by practice at home than by preachments abroad and that remonstrances to sovereign states made in private are usually more remunerative than public rebukes.

This discussion of the effect of foreign and domestic goals on national security serves as a reminder of the critical importance for the leadership of a country to choose the right goals at the outset and avoid the serious consequences to national interests resulting from errors in choice or from subsequent failure in execution. There are few risks for a government in endorsing general concepts like peace, beauty, and justice, but the dangers may be serious in adopting more specific objectives, such as those set forth in the Truman Doctrine which pledged us to the unconditional support of "free people who are resisting attempted subjugation by armed minorities or by outside pressures." Approved by a large congressional majority, the Truman Doctrine provided the basic justification for our policy in Indochina, which subsequent American opinion first questioned, then castigated, and finally disavowed with tragic consequences for ourselves and our allies.

There is usually a high price to pay if we decide to turn back from a course of action after the first step has been taken, a price paid in terms of discredited leadership, loss of international respect, injury to allies who joined us in the enterprise, and humiliation at home. As Voltaire remarked concerning the difficulties of Saint Denis in walking from the scene of his martyrdom carrying his severed head in his hands, "It is the first step that counts." How can our leaders always be sure of the rightness of their first step?

Our recent experience in Southeast Asia suggests that gross errors can be avoided if we take more time to analyze the legitimacy of the national interest that leads us to take the critical first step. Suppose, for example, our government were to consider a unilateral guarantee of the survival of Israel, carrying with it a promise to commit United States military forces in the Mideast if necessary. If our officials remembered the effect of inadequate information on Indochina policy, they would take a hard look at the adequacy of their information regarding the political and economic situation in Israel, the attitude of our NATO allies toward our proposed guarantee, the possibility of getting other countries to join with us, the reaction to be expected from the USSR, and the support or opposition anticipated at home. In such a case, the information at hand would probably be found inadequate and the President of the moment, like Truman in 1950 at the time of the invasion of South Korea or Kennedy in 1961 when he decided to reinforce the American effort in Vietnam, would be faced with the dilemma of making a critical decision without all the facts, or running the risk of inaction while awaiting information that might never come.

Even while wrestling with such a choice, a president should make some effort with the information available to appraise the gains to be hoped from success, the cost and probability of success, and the added cost that failure or inaction would entail. If it turned out later that the United States guarantee without requiring military involvement had provided ample protection for Israel and had avoided a renewal of the Mideast war, the gains would be obvious and substantial—the elimination, at least for the moment, of a threat to world peace and of the danger of a military confrontation with the USSR;

the establishment of some degree of stability in a former locus of trouble; and added prestige for American leadership.

The cost of such success would be difficult to quantify in advance, but it would be considerable. American support of Israel in this form, even without military intervention, would incur deep Arab resentment, possibly accompanied by a new resort to the oil weapon for reprisals against us and our friends. The latter would be critical of our actions if we brought new hardships upon them or upon Japan. Our home front would be equally unhappy if Arab reprisals caused additional domestic discomforts. Our success might lead the Soviets to give more weapons to Arab states, thus encouraging them to continue their vendetta against Israel at some later time. The degree of security thus achieved for Israel might not be sufficient to relieve it from the economic burden of continuing at least partial mobilization.

If these would be some of the costs of success, what about the probability and cost of failure? It is not difficult to conceive of many obstacles and contingencies which might arise to thwart our purpose. There is the danger that the Israelis, encouraged by our guarantee, might commit provocations against their Arab neighbors, thus damaging their case in international eyes and undermining our efforts to achieve a lasting peace. Political feuding within Israel, accompanied by growing economic problems, could reduce Israeli capacity for self-defense. Under the circumstances, we could hardly expect any other nation to join in underwriting our guarantee and sharing our obligation. If our guarantee alone proved inadequate to stay further Arab attacks, we would have to make good on our promise to deploy forces to Israel unless Congress, under the terms of the War Powers Act, withheld the necessary statutory authority or ordered our troops back after sixty days.

There would be considerable reason for Congress to take such action. If this contingency arose in the near future, it would find American ground forces still critically short of much of the combat equipment transferred to Israel after the autumn campaign of 1973. If fighting broke out or seemed imminent, it would be necessary to revive the draft in the United States, since volunteering is an uncertain source of military manpower when the shooting starts. This prospect might cause Congress to delay or halt any direct military involvement despite a previous political commitment.

Even if Congress approved the sending of combat troops to the defense of Israel, there would be no certainty of ultimate success. There would be serious logistical problems in getting forces and supplies from the United States to the area of conflict, even if they were available at home. There would be uncertainty about transit rights for U.S. aircraft flying to the Mideast. NATO might again object to the transfer of American troops and equipment from Europe. It is even possible that by this time one or more of the Arab states might have acquired submarines to complicate supply by sea. As in the case of Korea and Vietnam, once our forces were in the Mideast there would always be the question of how and when to disengage. Finally, at some point we might find ourselves confronted with Soviet forces and the possibility of the use of nuclear weapons by some participant.

As for the costs of failure after military intervention, they would include disaster for Israel, a serious blow to any future American role in this region, and a political storm at home. Even momentary success might be illusory and end in failure if one considers the growing military and economic strength of Israel's enemies and the increasing disparity in overall strength as the years pass.

In trying to evaluate the probable gains, costs, and risks, I doubt that our leaders would be able to strike a precise balance for or against the enterprise. The evaluation of the various factors and the assignment of a correct weight to each are matters of judgment requiring wisdom and experience, preferably including some acquaintance with the personality and character of allied and opposing leaders. In any case, I would say that the odds certainly would not look sufficiently favorable to warrant rushing singlehandedly into such a commitment with a light heart.

This brief excursion into Mideast policy has been to illustrate the kind of preliminary analysis that should take place before a president nails the flag of the country to an unsteady mast from which it cannot be lowered without serious consequences. Except possibly in the case of the Cuban missile crisis, I know of no instance when our leaders have made any such deliberate analysis of probable gains and losses before embarking on a dangerous course of action. The choice of goal, the survival of Israel, would seem to most of us a laudable objective; but it would be irresponsible to adopt it without a thorough understanding of all its possible implications. Instinct or hunch is a dangerous basis for decision in matters of such vital importance not only to our own security but often to that of friends as well.

III

Power in Support of National Security

In addition to the state of the future environment and the nature of the national policies which we are likely to pursue, a third determinant of the size and content of a feasible national security policy is the magnitude and type of the power resources which will be available to the President, directly or contingently, for this purpose.

Broadly speaking, the resources that may support national security come from four original sources: the Presidency, Congress, the economy, and the people. The Presidency contributes leadership, organization, policies, and the ways and means for executing the laws. Congress contributes laws, appropriations, and grants of authority to the president. The economy—the nation at work—produces food, goods, services, capital, and jobs to satisfy domestic demand; the equipment needed by the armed forces; the means for waging economic warfare; and, when possible, a surplus of goods for export. The people provide the popular support essential for national unity of effort; the human resources required by the government, the economy, and the armed forces; and the taxes needed to pay the bills. By their individual political activities as voters and officeholders, they make possible democratic government.

As a President surveys the power that these sources generate, he readily perceives that while he has direct call on a certain amount of the output, the availability of most forms of power is contingent upon external factors over which he has limited control. At his immediate disposition are the prestige of his high office, the support of the White House staff, and the professional advice of such bodies as the cabinet, the National Security Council, the Joint Chiefs of Staff, the Office of Management and Budget and the Economic Policy Board. He is served by a far-flung intelligence community which provides him with information, forecasts, warnings, and estimates to guide his decisions and plans in the field of foreign policy. He has direct call on the diplomatic resources of the State Department and of the many government missions abroad. As Commander in Chief he exercises direct command over powerful armed forces ready to do his bidding in peace or war.

Although the foregoing resources may be regarded as directly and immediately available to the President, in fact he is not without restraints on his freedom to use them. These restraints increase as we pass to a consideration of the power derived from other sources farther removed from the purview of his authority. Consider, for example, the limitations imposed on a President in using the armed forces, in drawing on the economy, or in rallying public support for the purposes of national security.

In the case of the armed forces, their effectiveness in contributing to national security depends very heavily on Congress, which provides funds for their needs, regulates their size, equipment, and organization, and influences the course of the national policy which they reinforce. Beyond these traditional constraints, by the War Powers Act passed in 1973 over a Presidential veto, Congress has asserted a right to intervene in the making of war and the conduct of military operations to a degree unknown in this country since the days of the Articles of Confederation. The potential impact of this act on national security and the role of the armed forces is such as to warrant extended discussion at this point.

The first thing worthy of note in the War Powers Act is that Congress justifies its passage by the "necessary and proper" clause of Article I, Section 8, of the Constitution, which gives Congress the power

To make all Laws which shall be necessary and proper for carrying into Execution the foregoing Powers [of the Congress], and all other Powers vested by this Constitution in the Government of the United States, or in any Department or Officer thereof.

Basing its action on this clause, Congress drafted the War Powers Act as a legislative means to limit certain war powers exercised in the past by the President by defining his powers narrowly and prescribing their detailed execution.

The act accomplishes this limitation in two general ways. First, by the language of Sections 2 and 8 it restricts the President's independent authority to introduce troops in hostilities or to send them into situations where involvement in hostilities is clearly indicated solely to "a national emergency created by an attack upon the United States, its territories or possessions or its armed forces."* Under these terms, a President would have to seek a declaration of war or a congressional authorization before using the armed forces to protect citizens or their property abroad, before going to the aid of an ally under attack or threatened by attack, or before sending reinforcements to American units already deployed in a potential combat area. Had the act been in existence in 1950, President Truman would have been obliged to await congressional action before sending troops into South Korea—or violate the law. President Kennedy would have faced the same dilemma in the Cuban missile crisis with regard to sending military aircraft or reconnaissance missions over Cuba or establishing a naval quarantine around the island. Had he requested congressional authority, he would have lost the precious advantage of surprise which was so vital to success in frustrating Khrushchev's rash venture.

If a President without a declaration of war decides to send forces into a combat zone in a national emergency of the kind described in the act or even in quiet times sends abroad troops equipped for

---

*It may be argued that Section 2 of the act, which contains this language, is introductory in nature and not legally binding on a President. Nevertheless, it is a clear statement of congressional intent which, if ignored, could expose a President to retaliatory actions by Congress. Moreover, Section 8 reiterates the will of Congress in an unmistakable fashion.

combat, he becomes subject to a second set of restraints. He must report promptly to Congress what he has done, his authority therefore, and the estimated scope and duration of the hostilities or involvement. Thereafter, until Congress declares war or gives him statutory authorization, the President must be ready to withdraw the forces within sixty days unless he determines that their safety requires an extension to ninety days. However, at any time whatsoever, Congress, by a concurrent resolution, may direct the withdrawal of the forces from action overseas if there has been no declaration of war or statutory authorization in the meantime.

In another interesting passage (Section 8, A1 and 2), the act makes clear that these restrictions on the introduction of American forces into combat-related situations apply regardless of contrary language in former provisions of law or in any treaty heretofore or hereafter ratified unless the treaty provision is implemented by legislation specifically authorizing the introduction of U.S. forces. This language casts doubt upon the automaticity of an American military response to an armed attack on NATO allies, an action that we have agreed to regard as an attack on ourselves and to be resisted by all necessary actions, including the use of armed force.

What may be the combined effect of these provisions on the ability of the armed forces to discharge their tasks? While I am far from sure that I interpret the act precisely in accordance with the intended meaning of its authors, I find many causes for serious concern. Compliance with the provisions requiring prior congressional action introduces a factor of delay which could be fatal in many situations. One must bear in mind that this delay cannot be avoided by independent Presidential action unless the target of enemy attack is "the United States, its territories or possessions, or its Armed Forces." Yet many of our national valuables fall outside this restricted list—our citizens and their possessions abroad;* allies like NATO, South

---

*It may be said that a President as Chief Executive is justified in using the armed forces overseas to protect U.S. citizens and property in the discharge of his responsibility for the faithful execution of the laws. But even so, such an action on a significant scale could be regarded as a subterfuge designed to circumvent the clear intent of Congress to prevent further "Presidents' wars" without formal congressional approval.

Korea, and the Organization of American States; friends like Israel; sources of important raw materials like Saudi Arabia, Nigeria, South Africa, and Indonesia; and important straits like Malacca, Sunda, Hormuz, and Bab el Mandeb which control large amounts of world shipping.

Our present overseas deployments might at any time find themselves in a situation where hostilities appeared imminent. They are where they are under the terms of treaties and understandings, which in effect commit them to join in resisting armed aggression whether or not the American units are themselves directly attacked. There has been no specific legislation authorizing them to be in their present locations. What do they do if the allied front is attacked somewhere outside their sector? Do they await a declaration of war or some special congressional authorization to enter combat? Must the President also await congressional action before sending them reinforcements? These are some of the troublesome, unanswerable questions raised by this piece of legislation.

A related cause for concern arises from the provision of the act which allows Congress, by a concurrent resolution, to withdraw forces from combat if they are abroad without a declaration of war or specific statutory authorization. This condition would exist today if fighting broke out in NATO or in Korea where we have troops already deployed. As I read the act, upon the outbreak of hostilities Congress could order these forces to withdraw forthwith and return to the United States regardless of the treaty arrangements under which they have previously operated.

The consultation and reporting to Congress required under various situations are likely to result in a premature revelation of political intentions and military plans, restricting the President's ability to threaten credibly the use of military force. The movement of units of the Sixth Fleet to the eastern Mediterranean, a common reaction in the past to renewed Arab-Israeli tensions, would presumably require prior congressional action if hostilities were deemed imminent. An overall consequence of the act could be a dulling of the deterrent effectiveness of our armed forces—one of the prime reasons for their existence.

If a primary purpose of the act is to discourage any President from making undeclared war, it is likely to be successful. A declaration of war would void many of the objections raised against it provided the situation permitted the time required to obtain one. Many students of the Vietnam war are of the opinion that President Johnson would have moderated much of the antiwar sentiment had he obtained a declaration of war in lieu of the Tonkin Gulf resolution. Most Americans still feel that a declaration of war effects a profound change in the responsibilities of a citizen to his government—a sentiment that a President may wish henceforth to exploit in the interest of national unity whenever military operations are imminent or in progress. Given the additional advantage of forcing Congress to share responsibility for sending troops into combat, a future President is likely to seek a declaration of war in any case unless the time factor does not permit delay or a declaration is inappropriate or inadvisable. We would hardly have been warranted in declaring war to legitimize the bloodless Lebanon landing in 1958, the intervention in the Dominican Republic in 1965, or the recent *Mayaguez* incident of May, 1975. Objections of a different nature dissuaded the Johnson administration from seeking a declaration of war against North Vietnam. In this case, certain of the President's advisers felt that a strong possibility existed of a mutual defense treaty between Hanoi and Peking or Hanoi and Moscow which might become operative if the United States declared war on any one of the parties.

In the light of the foregoing considerations, the War Powers Act appears to me to be one that imposes serious restraints, some of them probably unconstitutional, upon the President in discharging his duties as Commander in Chief. If so, should not the Executive branch take prompt action to challenge its constitutionality in the courts rather than put off a showdown until a crisis is at hand demanding prompt Presidential action? It is easy to argue that it is untimely to open a new jurisdictional conflict between the White House and Congress and alarm our allies to no avail over the delay in American military reaction implicit in the act—after all, they have only recently been exposed to the shock of American failure in Southeast Asia.

Also, I have heard the view expressed that a President needing to act promptly will ignore the law and do the right thing as he sees it—so why worry about the act?

One may derive some support for the latter attitude from the *Mayaguez* incident, during which President Ford probably violated two laws in the course of freeing our ship and crew from the Cambodians. He certainly introduced United States military forces into a potential combat situation overseas in the absence of a declaration of war, a statutory authorization, or anything approaching a national emergency as defined by the War Powers Act. Furthermore, he appears to have violated the statute that prohibited American military activity of any kind in Indochina after August 15, 1973. Despite these two legal bars, President Ford elected to take drastic military action with minimal congressional consultation—an initiative which had the saving grace of success in liberating both ship and sailors. For so doing, he received national acclaim and very little criticism from Congress.

I would submit, however, that it is unfair to any future President to expect him to bear the consequences of violating the law in order to do his duty as Commander in Chief, particularly if he runs a high risk of failure. Remembering the defense of the Vietnam war protesters, draft dodgers, and military deserters that their conduct was vindicated because the war was illegal, he could anticipate serious trouble in maintaining order at home and discipline in the armed forces if he could be fairly charged with taking military action in violation of the War Powers Act. Nixon's narrow escape from impeachment would remind him of the real possibility of that form of retribution for future Presidents who take the law into their own hands.

For these reasons I regard the War Powers Act as far too important a piece of legislation to put aside and hope that its potential for mischief will never be realized in practice. If its provisions are carried out in the way they are apparently meant, they will impose a serious limitation of the powers of the Commander in Chief. If a President willfully violates them in time of emergency, he will create a major issue to divide popular opinion at a time when national unity is essential. To prevent either eventuality from taking place at a critical moment in history, the Executive branch should challenge the law in the courts, preferably at a time when the issue can be considered with relative composure.

Having noted the limitations imposed on the President in the use of the armed forces, we may now consider the availability of economic means in support of national security.

In normal times, the first task of the economy is to satisfy the domestic demand for food, goods, services, jobs, and profits while maintaining the standard of living at acceptable levels. In the past it has usually succeeded not only in satisfying these domestic needs but in producing a surplus of products for export which has been both an economic and a political asset. In time of war, the economy has displayed great flexibility in adapting its output to the requirements, American and allied, for arms and equipment while still meeting essential civilian needs. In both peace and war, it affords means for waging offensive and defensive economic warfare if Congress authorizes and the country supports such measures.

Although the economy is a potential source of power in the support of national security, ordinarily there are many restrictions upon its use for any such purpose. As we all know, it is a private economy owned primarily by private citizens, not by the government. Although many government agencies have responsibility for supervising or promoting some aspect of its many functions—the Departments of the Treasury, Commerce, Agriculture, the Interior, Labor, and Transportation, to mention a few—their authority to intervene actively is limited by the terms of congressional legislation. Within the Executive branch, such authority over it as exists is widely diffused with no one short of the President responsible for coordinating all related activities. Hence, when a complex issue such as the energy crisis arises, it has been past practice for the President to scurry about to find a "czar" to put in charge of a task force, usually composed of strangers assembled overnight to cope with the unexpected danger. Although we decided long ago against reliance on minutemen and "shirt-sleeve heroes" to resist military attack, we still have no reluctance to depend on their counterparts to withstand threats to our economic well-being.

Since 1973, we have suffered from economic aggression conducted by the OPEC cartel which has threatened to undermine the free-enterprise system world-wide. Yet the President lacks freedom of action to respond promptly in kind by using to the fullest in reprisal such potent economic weapons as control of access to the American market; the regulation of foreign investments in the United States; the limitation of American exports of advanced technology, managerial skills, food, fertilizers, and materials of strategic importance; and the granting or withholding of most-favored-nation status in world trade. To do such things it is necessary first to obtain congressional approval, a matter which always requires time. The Ninety-third Congress spent two years debating the trade bill of 1974 giving the President authority to reduce trade barriers in preparation for world-wide trade negotiations. While its passage was complicated by the issue of Jewish emigration from the USSR, such bills have a way of accumulating extraneous amendments which delay their passage.

In the light of these obstacles, it will be difficult for national security planners to count on the ready use of economic tools to coerce opponents except in time of war or serious national emergency. At such times in the past, Congress has been inclined to give blanket powers to the President that have permitted the waging of effective economic warfare. But in lesser crises, Congress has been very cautious in granting special Presidential authority in this area of high political sensitivity. Any expansion of governmental planning in economic matters raises the bugbear of government in business and a controlled economy.

Earlier, I stressed the importance of public support as a prerequisite to Presidential success in assuring national security. However, this form of power is an uncertain asset because of the notorious volatility of American opinion, as is frequently demonstrated in opinion polls. Oddly, despite the vast personal publicity he receives, a President has limited means to assist him in favorably influencing public opinion toward his policies.

Most other governments engage in opinion-molding activities of various sorts, ranging from advertisements of tourist attractions to propaganda of varying degrees of violence and often extending to overt forms of press control. In the United States, where anything smacking of propaganda or encroachment on a free press is inherently obnoxious and where the media reject being "used" in any way to promote government themes, a President has only the United States Information Agency as an institutional advocate for his policies—an advocacy which is restricted by law to the overseas public. Otherwise he must depend largely on his own gifts of persuasion reinforced by those of political associates and hope to obtain occasional prime TV time from the networks to explain his case before a national audience.

In this competition for the public ear, he will have aligned against him his political opponents and a majority of the influential voices of press, radio, and television. Whereas he can work at the task only intermittently, they oppose him pretty much around the clock. In the long run the odds are against him to get an even break unless he can develop the personal appeal of a Franklin Roosevelt in a fireside chat.

Thus far we have considered the constraints imposed on some of the forms of power that the President might desire to use on behalf of national security. But even if all restraints on Presidential authority were removed or considerably relaxed, there would still be the problem of needless loss of Executive power which might otherwise be available. The Executive branch can be compared to a generator rated to produce a certain horsepower but actually delivering much less because of internal friction and inefficiency of design. Add to this condition a team of inexperienced engineers recently employed to operate the machine who are still uncertain of the location of its valves, brakes, and gauges, and we would have a reasonably exact analogy of Executive difficulties in power generation—particularly at the start of a new administration.

Losses of power may also result from the expenditure of resources for wrong purposes, from ill-conceived or badly executed programs, or from inadequacies of government organization. Elsewhere we have noted the costliness of choosing wrong goals for national policy; we can also waste resources in retaining outmoded national interests which have lost their validity. The prolonged dedication of the Kennedy and Johnson administrations to the Truman Doctrine in the belief that the country was still committed to the containment of communism is an example of a one-time national interest that had overstayed its time. To avoid this kind of self-delusion, there should be a recurrent review of national interests and related commitments to verify that a majority of our citizens are still willing to endure hardships in their name.

Waste of power may also result from internal frictions arising from interbranch and interdepartmental jealousies and jurisdictional squabbles—the White House versus Congress, the State Department versus the NSC staff, the Central Intelligence Agency versus the Federal Bureau of Investigation, or Army versus Navy versus Air Force. Our carefully designed system of checks and balances works very well as long as there is a cooperative spirit among the major elements of government; but these protective devices may be abused to the frustration and stalemate of vital governmental functions.

We may also waste power by giveaways to adversaries while getting an inadequate return. In negotiations at the end of both the Korean and Vietnam wars, our government was guilty of wasting political and military advantages gained at great cost through unreciprocated concessions. In the Paris negotiations, we allowed the North Vietnamese representatives to reject as immoral every American claim that they owed us something in return for ceasing the introduction of American troops and for stopping the bombing of North Vietnam. We have never learned to wage negotiations in the unrelenting spirit of our Communist adversaries and, as a result, have often lost a good part of the national shirt at the peace table.

I have already alluded to some of the forms of personnel ineffi-ciency that contribute to power loss. Inexperienced and untrained officials in high places are a very common cause of poor governmental performance. Somewhere in our past, we Americans have acquired a conviction that any citizen regardless of background who can get elected or appointed to office is automatically qualified at once to perform its functions. The corollary to this belief is that the long-time government expert is a man of small ambition who, having neither carried a precinct nor met a payroll, could never be a success in private life. So while civil service has replaced the spoils system in filling junior and intermediate federal positions, senior jobs are still patronage perquisites to be filled by transient incumbents who come and go with the tide of partisan politics.

With such an influx of amateurs, one might expect to find an established procedure for helping newcomers adjust to their unfamiliar responsibilities. Unfortunately, such is not the case. In most new administrations it has been a matter of party pride for the new arrivals of the incoming team to throw out all the "old rascals" along with their files and, more importantly, their secretaries, who know all the important telephone numbers without which a new bureaucrat is helpless. Thus there are virtually no old-timers about other than civil-service employees to explain the ropes to the newcomers.

Even if old hands were available, many new officials would be reluctant to ask questions that might expose their ignorance of the government machine for which they are responsible and would tend to react in one of two ways. Lacking self-confidence, they might become timid in making decisions and thereby delay the flow of business; or, alternatively, they might display an unjustified assurance conducive to blunders which foul up the business. With such conditions existing in many offices of the Executive, the newcomers devote much of the first year to on-the-job self-training, which leaves little time to learn coordinated teamplay with their colleagues. It is a perilous time for the Republic during which patriotic citizens should utter an occasional prayer for preservation from another Bay of Pigs or worse.

As a cause for loss of power, official ineptitude may be compounded by inadequacies of governmental organization and an absence of procedures to deal with the complex problems of the day. The Executive branch is an organizational monstrosity of some sixty departments, agencies, and offices reporting in parallel lines to the White House desk where, as President Truman said, "the buck stops." It has been compared to an overgrown pipe organ to which rich donors keep adding pipes but no console to permit the organist to orchestrate them. The confusion of the organization often discourages senior officials—even Presidents—from trying to use it when in a hurry, and reinforces the tendency to meet a new problem by creating an *ad hoc* committee which, after submitting a paper on the subject assigned, disappears without leaving a trace to guide posterity. Such disorganization complicates the translation of Presidential decisions into specific tasks when several Executive agencies are responsible for doing a piece of a large project. Even if jobs are correctly assigned, since a President has no field inspectors of his own to send about the world to verify the fulfillment of his orders, the follow-up on Presidential decisions is usually weak or nonexistent. To know how his subordinates are doing, he must depend on their own reports on themselves, on the news he receives from the media, or on investigations initiated by Congress.

We have had recent evidence attesting to the inadequacy of this jerry-built Executive structure to cope with multidepartmental issues such as inflation, energy, foreign aid, environmental protection, and hostile cartels on the model of OPEC. The Executive has no in-house centers for continuous study and research of such problems analogous to the medical research conducted by the National Institutes of Health in the Department of Health, Education, and Welfare. Also, it contains no operational units able to assume undivided responsibility for the execution of a master program dealing with something like energy. In contrast to governmental readiness to plan and execute in the foreign/military field, on the civil side of the Executive branch the President must often depend on improvisations conducted by unprepared officials supported by untrained staffs.

A final factor contributing to the loss of power is the absence of something corresponding to the National Security Council in the nonmilitary field. But even if a duplicate were constructed to deal with civil problems, the President would still have no single forum where he and his senior advisers could survey the whole range of national policy and establish priorities between competing programs contending for essentially the same resources. As we have remarked, with time foreign policy and domestic policy have come to blend together, as have the distinctions between national security and national well-being. Until there exists a single central forum which can survey and coordinate all national policy from the formative stage onward, a large quantity of potential national power will remain untapped and the nonmilitary sector of our national security will continue to be a vulnerable, exposed front.

IV

The Vietnam Defeat
and National Security

In the course of writing this book, an unexpected event occurred which is certain to have both short- and long-term effects on our security and the power available to support it. In April, 1975, the armed forces of South Vietnam collapsed with little warning before a renewed Communist offensive in the northern and northwest provinces, bringing down in defeat an American policy of two decades. Although President Thieu and his military leaders bore the direct responsibility for the disorderly troop withdrawal which ended in chaos and the disintegration of the forces, the United States shared in the disaster by virtue of long participation in the strategy which failed and the effects of various actions taken by the President and Congress during and after the so-called cease-fire of January, 1973. These actions demoralized our allies and contributed to the conditions which led President Thieu to withdraw his forces and yield the northern provinces to the enemy.

The counts against our government are at least four in number. To get Thieu's agreement to a cease-fire, we pressured him into accepting the Big Lie, propagated by Hanoi, that there were no North Vietnamese troops in South Vietnam to be withdrawn under the terms of the cease-fire. Actually all parties knew that there were about 150,000 such troops in the northwest provinces of South Vietnam, ready to serve as a bridgehead in support of a new offensive after the departure of the American forces.

To obtain Thieu's acquiescence to this dangerous concession, President Nixon and Dr. Kissinger promised our allies that we would continue indefinitely the military and economic assistance necessary to assure the continued defense of South Vietnam if the war were resumed. To this assurance, President Nixon added a strong intimation of our intention to retaliate militarily if the cease-fire broke down as a result of Hanoi action.

Meanwhile, however, Watergate disclosures had brought Congress into such violent conflict with Nixon and his White House staff that the legislators were in no mood to honor Nixon promises or to continue to support his Vietnam policy. As a belated assertion of authority, Congress took two actions which in combination removed all chance of success for South Vietnam in resisting the massive offensive that Hanoi was preparing. First, it passed an act prohibiting the involvement of American forces in any form of combat in Indochina after August 15, 1973, and thus relieved Hanoi of any fear of American military retaliation for renewing the war. By a subsequent congressional action, the military aid recommended for South Vietnam by the administration was reduced by $700,000,000, a sum that, despite entreaties, President Ford never succeeded in getting restored. President Thieu, recognizing that a total end of American aid was merely a matter of time, began to impose severe rationing of ammunition and gasoline on his forces, which sharply curtailed their operations at a time when they were heavily engaged in resisting an enemy offensive. Shortly thereafter, he further concluded that he must yield territory in the north to be able to protect the populous south and issued the disastrous order to withdraw that ended in the loss of his army, his capital, and the country.

With this record, historians will have grounds to charge the American government with culpability on the following points: Executive overeagerness to get a worthless cease-fire agreement at the expense of an ally; Executive overreadiness to make promises to an ally without obtaining prior congressional concurrence; congressional action in stripping President Nixon of reprisal weapons without which he could not credibly threaten retaliation; congressional refusal to give Presidentially promised aid to an ally in grave danger who might otherwise have survived. On TV screens, the world witnessed the immediate consequences—thousands of South Vietnamese fleeing for their lives before victorious Communist forces without an American friend in sight to help them.

Regardless of how one views the degree of American responsibility in this debacle, there can be little disagreement as to the magnitude of the defeat of American policy and the resultant damage to many sources of strength upon which our security depends. Loss of confidence in American protection became visible at once in Asian countries nearest the disaster area. Laos rapidly succumbed to total Communist control, another domino to lie beside Cambodia, already fallen. Thailand demanded the withdrawal of American forces as a step toward accommodation with Communist neighbors. Indications began to appear that our continued military presence in the Philippines was no longer welcome and that soon our military bases in the Far East might be reduced to those in Korea and Japan. Such a contraction would be most unfortunate since we have important interests in the oil and raw materials of Southeast Asia, Australia, and Indonesia, an area of the world that needs the stabilizing presence of some American forces, if only in token numbers.

If at the outset Korea and Japan showed no visible signs of wavering in their relations with the United States, that fact did not imply indifference to the weakened American posture in the Far East. Seoul promptly dispatched numerous senior officials to Washington to obtain renewed guarantees of American military support should the events in Vietnam encourage North Korea to violate the 1953 cease-fire. While President Ford and Secretary Kissinger gave robust assurances of American steadfastness to friends world-wide, they could not safely go beyond the text of treaties which pledge the United States to act to meet a common danger "in accordance with its constitutional processes." The latter phrase would now presumably embrace compliance with the terms of the War Powers Act of 1973.

While Tokyo leaders prudently kept their own counsel, they were undoubtedly weighing the future value of the United States–Japan Treaty of Mutual Cooperation and Security in the light of the changed situation in Southeast Asia. Elsewhere, we have already mentioned the possible attractions of a Japanese-Soviet *détente* promising political, economic, and military advantages. There is now an increased danger that the Japanese might decide to rearm to assure their self-defense if the American retreat from Asia seems likely to continue. If their rearmament should extend to nuclear weapons, it would create deep concern in many quarters of Asia, stimulate further proliferation elsewhere, and have unpredictable consequences on Japanese relations with the other great powers.

Our NATO allies foresee dangers to Western Europe in this decline of American prestige and reputation for reliability. Already troubled by inflation and high oil prices, and weakened politically and militarily by developments in Greece, Turkey, and Portugal, the Western European countries are deeply worried by signs of neoisolationism appearing in America and recurrent rumors of a major reduction of U.S. forces in Europe. Israel is particularly sensitive to the American postwar mood which seems to reject the thought of military intervention for anybody anywhere. It senses that the American defeat may influence our behavior in one of two quite different directions. In an effort to re-establish a reputation for tough virility, American leaders may be inclined to promise more to Israel than they can deliver. Or, in deference to the isolationist attitude at home and the uncertainty of sustained popular support for a hard-line Mideast policy which risks a new oil embargo, they may tend to hypercaution and timidity. In any case, American performance of commitments to allies in Southeast Asia will make the Israelis want holographic promises of unqualified support from the President endorsed by Congress before compromising their security by further concessions to the Arabs.

It would appear at the moment that a principal casualty of the Vietnam defeat has been the American posture of strength, always regarded as an essential adjunct of national security. It has suffered particularly from the impression of a weakened President emerging from the conflict with Congress over primacy in foreign policy and directive authority over the armed forces. Whereas the outside world had become accustomed to view the President as the chief artisan of our foreign policy and an unchallenged Commander in Chief in the conduct of war, declared or undeclared, now that image is blurred.

Since its heady triumph in reversing American policy in Southeast Asia, Congress has made a series of new interventions in the conduct of foreign relations with discouraging results. The record indicates that it botched the 1975 trade bill by interjecting the extraneous issue of Jewish emigrations from the USSR, and alienated our most important Mediterranean ally, Turkey, by suspending military aid because of Turkish policy in Cyprus. A large majority of the Senate, by public espousal of the Israeli cause, seriously impaired the American position as a fair-handed mediator in the Mideast conflict. As already noted, by the War Powers Act Congress has claimed the right not only to declare war but to direct or intervene in military operations. It is not surprising if foreign leaders wonder who is in charge in Washington.

In the gloom following the fall of Saigon, the *Mayaguez* incident brought an unexpected ray of sunshine so timely as to stir suspicion that it had been somehow contrived. Congress, for the moment, abandoned its adversary attitude toward the White House, accepted without complaint a highly elastic interpretation of its own interdiction against further military operations in Indochina, and joined in presenting a refreshing picture of national unity. In the outcome, it appeared that the country had once more fulfilled its historic commitment to the principle of freedom of the seas and its obligation to protect our ships from acts of piracy. National morale went up and there was hope expressed that the incident had redeemed our unheroic behavior in Vietnam and had restored our standing in the international community.

But it required only a short time to dissipate much of this optimism. Clearly, the episode was not to be compared to the Battle of Midway, which paid off many of the scores of Pearl Harbor; it was more like the Doolittle air raid on Tokyo. That gallant action did little damage to Tokyo, but, as the first success after a long string of defeats, it momentarily electrified the discouraged Western nations fighting for their lives against the Axis powers. While the *Mayaguez* affair may have restored some vitality to our drooping morale at the time, it would take a sustained performance of national duty under far more difficult circumstances to erase the Vietnam record of failure.

It is still too early to pass final judgment on the effects of our loss in Vietnam. In the first six months following the fall of Saigon there were surprisingly few public voices raised to deplore the loss of 17 million South Vietnamese to the Communist domination from which we had promised them protection. Meantime, many of the American political leaders who had urged most strongly the withdrawal of our support from Vietnam became the most vociferous advocates of a commitment to the even more precarious cause of 4 million Israelis.

Before taking any such a step, we should meditate on the losses in world respect, reputation, and influence that we have suffered in Vietnam. Many of our alliances are weakened; important overseas bases and logistic facilities have become insecure; and the range of our political and military options has been sharply reduced. Although our armed forces were never defeated in battle in Vietnam, they have lost much in their deterrent effectiveness—a quality that depends not merely on military strength but on the quality of national leaders and on the popular support they enjoy. For the moment, at least, our will to use military power is a matter of doubt. In the light of these losses, it would seem prudent to go slow in undertaking new foreign commitments until we have had time to regroup our forces, recoup some of our losses, and reflect on the experience acquired in a defeat largely of our own doing. One lesson that I hope we have learned is the need to bring our rash and often self-destructive impulses under control and to concentrate on restoring the national unity which has been a primary victim of the Vietnam war and its tragic ending.

We should now be ready to outline a national security policy consistent with the broadened concept of security that we have advocated and the requirements of the future environment insofar as they can be foreseen. It should be one that is adequate to support the likely goals of national policy and that is assured of the necessary resources to carry out its purposes. Such a policy must give due regard to the growing importance of economic and environmental factors and the need to strengthen the unorganized and undeveloped forms of nonmilitary power, particularly that derivable from our economic strength. But while improving the defenses of the civil sector, we cannot neglect the continued maintenance of strong armed forces to offset the expanding Soviet military power, contribute stability to great power relations, and allay the turbulence which we must anticipate in the have-not world.

In these tasks we shall need all possible help from friends and allies. But, unhappily, many of our present alliances appear irrelevant to our future needs and others have been seriously weakened by the debility of member states. In a redesign of national security policy we must determine what we shall want abroad from friends and which countries can provide it.

At home we shall have our own internal weaknesses to worry about —defects already discernible which threaten to impair our future strength and create doubts as to our ability to continue a world leader. There are signs of inner decay which suggest dwindling national vitality and ebbing self-respect.

In considering measures to reinforce our national security at such a time I would rule out any that would require fundamental changes in our present structure of government. After all, the defense of the Constitution and the institutions springing from it remains a basic purpose of national security as we have conceived it. Hence, designers of a new national security policy should seek to adapt present governmental organization to new requirements with modifications of structure and procedure limited to those which, being evolutionary in nature, can be effected without constitutional amendments. The latter are necessarily time consuming and should be undertaken only after lesser measures have proved clearly inadequate.

With the foregoing points in mind, I shall outline the salient features of a national security program consisting of a military and a nonmilitary component. Because of the long and well-recorded experience of the military in contingency planning, force design, and mission execution, the treatment of the military component will be more detailed than that of its civil counterpart. Thus far, the latter has had an ill-defined role in national security and little opportunity to develop experience in multidepartmental planning and programming. Hence, in the civil field I shall limit my suggestions to ways for providing the organization and procedures needed to develop solutions and not undertake to advance the solutions themselves. In the meantime I am afraid that urgent current problems such as inflation and energy must continue to depend for resolution on improvised means as in the past.

V

The Military Component of the National Security Program

The first step in designing the military component of our national security program would be to determine what contribution the armed forces should make. My approach to such a determination would be to consider their potential in terms of their war-making function, their role in support of foreign and domestic policies, their contribution to a national posture of strength, and their obligation to use wisely and effectively the national resources allocated to them.

Their war-making function derives from the military force at their disposition for use in preventing war or waging war to a successful conclusion—that is, a conclusion that achieves the national objective in a conflict. While success in this sense will often require the destruction of the armed forces of the enemy, it may also be achieved by lesser means if they are adequate to break the enemy resistance to our national purpose. It is always possible that a wily diplomatic maneuver, the subversion of a hostile government, a barter of territory, a king's daughter given in marriage, or the subornation of a cabinet minister may remove a foreign obstacle from the path of national policy without resort to the *ultima ratio regis*. In the coming era, more sinister nonmilitary means may be invoked for this purpose

—blackmail based on threats to hostages, the use of nuclear weapons or chemical agents against civil populations, or the sabotage of public utilities essential to modern life—power, water, heat, or communications. International terrorism threatens to become an increasingly common means for political coercion.

I mention these alternative possibilities for breaking the will of an enemy to emphasize the recurrent point that there are potent non-military means which may be used to support or to substitute for armed forces in advancing a national cause. Nevertheless, the latter remain the ultimate weapon of legitimate governments for breaking the will of a stubborn enemy, and it is against their ability to perform that task that the adequacy of our armed forces should be measured. While this criterion will be a general determinant of their size and composition, force designers will be obliged also to take into account the kinds of warfare they must be prepared to wage.

On the latter point, our previous evaluation of the more likely dangers to be found in the future environment suggests a need to cope with three broad categories of warfare or armed violence. On the basis of their ultimate purpose, armed conflict may be regarded as total or limited; by the weapons and tactics employed, as strategic nuclear, tactical nuclear, conventional, or subversive; by their effect on the world power balance, as major or minor. A single conflict may have the attributes of more than one category.

Total war is just what the term implies—one in which country A at war with country B mobilizes and uses whatever means and resources are necessary and available to assure its own survival or to destroy or enforce the complete submission of B. The distinguishing characteristic of total war in this sense is that the political or physical survival of at least one of the participants is at stake.

All wars not "total" in the above sense may be termed *limited* for the purposes of our discussion. The fact is, of course, that all war is limited in some way. Constraints may be imposed by national war aims, by the size of the forces and kinds of weapons available for use by the military commanders, by the strategy approved by the political leadership, by the territorial boundaries set for the war zone, and by the enemy targets approved for attack. In an even broader sense, wars are further limited by the laws of nature, the vagaries of human behavior, and the characteristics of the terrain and the weather of the war zone. Time, space, and the state of science and technology may also play a part. Thus, total war escapes limitation only by the absolute nature of the war objective and the willingness of participants to pay any price and use any means to survive or succeed.

The kinds of weapons and tactics employed are the distinguishing mark of the second category of wars. The appearance of nuclear weapons at the end of World War II produced a feeling in the West, particularly in the United States, that the "absolute weapon" had been found which would bring an end to war as known in the past. Until about the time when *Sputnik I* demonstrated a possible Soviet capability to employ intercontinental missiles, the Eisenhower administration was convinced that the threat of massive retaliation would be sufficient to maintain a *Pax Americana* and eliminate the need for any substantial number of presumably outmoded conventional forces. The shock administered by *Sputnik* to American complacency generated a tremendous drive to develop long-range missiles which, in their present state of development, can reach European and Asian targets from launch silos in the United States and from submarines submerged at sea. Concurrently, we have retained a strategic bomber fleet of moderate size to provide a third delivery system for the megaton weapons now available for waging strategic war.

Another assumption of the early nuclear period was that small nuclear weapons were technologically infeasible and, even if they could be made, would be prohibitively expensive. But this assumption underestimated American technology and, by about 1960, had proved erroneous. At present, all American services have a large arsenal of tactical nuclear weapons for battlefield use, deliverable by rocket, airplane, and artillery piece, with a wide range of destructive effects. Thus it has become possible to conceive of an intermediate level of armed conflict between conventional and strategic warfare involving the battlefield use of tactical nuclear weapons concurrently with nonnuclear munitions. However, over the years, our commanders have never received official assurance of being able to count on the use of tactical nuclear weapons. The thought of using any kind of nuclear weapon with the ever-present possibility of uncontrolled escalation has been so repugnant to civil authorities as to preclude virtually any serious discussion of the possibility or the conditions under which these weapons might be used.

Despite forecasts of its consignment to the limbo of the Greek hoplite and the armored knight, conventional warfare remains an active possibility on the world scene—indeed, it is the only form of warfare that has been waged since the bombing of Nagasaki in 1945. Meanwhile, technology has continued to improve its weapons. Quite lately our conventional forces have been reinforced by new types of high-precision, "smart" weapons* particularly effective in destroying tanks, tactical aircraft, and point targets like bridges, radars, and communication centers. These weapons have proved their effectiveness both in Vietnam and in the Autumn campaign of 1973.

At a lower level of violence there is a catchall of subversive and paramilitary activities waged for political purposes with the weapons of the guerrilla, the saboteur, the terrorist, and the assassin. I would group this aggregate under the rather inadequate heading of subversive violence since the purpose is usually to subvert government authority, institutions, or civil order and thereby to undermine the status quo. The means employed, while often primitive, may extend to those of conventional warfare—one may even conceive of the use or threat of nuclear weapons obtained by illegal or clandestine means. As demonstrated in South Vietnam, the Greece civil war, and the Malayan insurgency, subversive violence has often been fomented and actively supported from foreign bases in an adjacent country. In Communist jargon, this technique became known as a "War of National Liberation" which was proclaimed in the early sixties as a cheap and sure way of extending Communist dominion over weak countries.

The third classification of possible wars stems from the global

---

*Known as precision-guided munitions (PGMs).

political effect of their outcome. A war in which a great power is a belligerent or one which for other reasons might upset the international power equilibrium is *major* in the eyes of world political leaders; those of lesser impact may be rated *minor*.

If we accept this glossary of terms as embracing war and armed violence in its various modern aspects, let us see how we would categorize recent conflicts with which we are all familiar. World War II was clearly a major war since it involved great powers and its outcome caused fundamental changes in the world power balance. It was also total for the principals who committed all their resources without stint and staked their survival as independent nations on the outcome.

The Korean War was a major war because the United States was involved; it was also a total war for South Korea since its survival was in danger. The war in South Vietnam is more difficult to categorize. From 1954 to 1959, it was a subversive conflict directed by North Vietnam but carried on largely by South Vietnamese insurgents. From 1959 to 1964 it remained subversive but, as North Vietnamese units began to appear on the battlefield, it assumed some of the characteristics of minor conventional war. After United States intervention with combat units, the war became major because the United States had become a belligerent and, as the Duke of Wellington reminded Parliament in 1838, "a great country cannot wage a little war." Even after the departure of American combat troops following the cease-fire, the war remained major because of the impact that the outcome was sure to have on American authority abroad and on politics at home. Throughout the long conflict, the South Vietnamese were fighting a total war with their national survival at stake.

The India-Pakistan-Bangladesh conflict in 1972 was a good example of a minor, limited war. The Middle East hostilities between Arabs and Israelis must be accounted a major war because of the part played by the United States and the USSR in backing opposing belligerents and the persistent danger to the stability of the Western nations in event of a new war accompanied by another oil embargo. The war is total for the Israelis, limited for their enemies. The activities of the Palestine Liberation Organization and the subsequent Israeli reprisals thereto have introduced an element of subversive violence.

If the foregoing categories represent the classes of war, our security planners would like to know which ones to prepare for and in what order of priority. In discussing the expected environment, we have tended to agree that although strategic nuclear war was the greatest disaster that one could contemplate, it also had a low order of probability; that major war involving great powers seemed unlikely but the possibility could not be excluded; and that minor conflicts were highly probable although difficult to predict as to time and place. After this more careful consideration of the possible forms of war, it may be worth our while to review the earlier appraisal to see if it requires modification.

A belief that strategic nuclear war is highly improbable rests on the disastrous consequences to victor and vanquished resulting from a general strategic exchange—indeed, the difficulty that would exist in distinguishing the one from the other. Since it has been presumed that the leaders of states capable of having strategic weapons will be rational beings committed to the well-being of their people and their own survival, one has felt justified in believing that they would be deterred from risking strategic warfare. In any case, up to now we have put our trust in the efficacy of deterrence.

The elements that make up deterrence will be examined when we set about designing a strategic retaliatory force capable of continuing to deter the USSR. For the moment, I am merely asserting the proposition that it seems a reasonably safe bet that strategic war can be deterred if certain conditions are met, which we shall shortly undertake to identify. I concede in advance that I know of no way to protect ourselves against the consequences of human error, of the mechanical failure of weapons, or of the acts of criminals or irrational men with access to these weapons.

As to the likelihood of major or minor war, one must assume the continued presence of motive forces which throughout history have been causes of war—fear, hatred, envy, greed, lust for power, dissatisfaction with the status quo, and the desire to divert domestic discontent to a foreign scapegoat. On a planet with shrinking resources and a vastly expanding population, the motivations for violence will be numerous and the chances for armed conflict very high. While major powers with less to gain and more to lose from war may be expected to opt for peace, they may have war forced upon them. But even if major powers are not participants, any outbreak of prolonged military conflict in this contracting world may disturb the world power balance and thus become a major war in the political sense.

In recent years, incidents of subversive violence have been matters of almost daily occurrence world-wide, with focal points in Northern Ireland, the Mideast, and certain Latin American countries. As was once claimed for "Wars of National Liberation," the violence of terrorist groups may prove the cheapest and safest way for disrupting the status quo and undermining governments, particularly in industrial countries especially vulnerable to sabotage.

If the armed forces are to be able to cope with these multiple forms of war and violence, we must give them the necessary manpower, weapons, and equipment to do the job. They must have strategic weapons and associated equipment which will maximize their ability to deter strategic nuclear war with primary concern for the threat of the USSR. Additionally, they must include conventional forces with tactical nuclear weapons at their disposal, capable of dealing quickly and effectively with conflicts which may otherwise develop into major or minor war or advanced forms of subversive violence. In the jargon of the Pentagon, these conventional forces are known as "general-purpose forces" since they have a broad range of employment in contrast with the highly specialized uses of strategic forces.

Obviously we will never have conventional forces in sufficient strength to "deal quickly and effectively" with every conflict with a potential for expansion. Some way must be found to concentrate our limited capabilities in those areas where the American interest is greatest or most exposed. Such areas include most of the Western Hemisphere, our principal trade partners and suppliers of vital raw materials in Europe and the Western Pacific, and the sea and air communications linking these areas to the United States. In some of these regions of special interest it will be desirable to maintain permanent bases and garrisons for a variety of purposes. For contingencies which cannot be predicted as to time or place, we shall need a ready central reserve in the United States from which forces can be dispatched abroad when their need becomes clear.

Forces with these capabilities would lend indispensable support to our foreign and domestic policies. By their visible strength and readiness, they contribute to the national posture of power and serve to reinforce the voice and hand of our political leaders. In the overseas areas where they are deployed, they serve as a symbol of American might and a stabilizing influence that encourages our allies. To assist the latter, our forces may provide equipment and training to the military elements of selected countries and provide many of their officers with instruction in our military school system. Over the years, tens of thousands of foreign officers have become proud alumni of American schools where they have formed career-long friendships with American classmates. After returning to their home countries, many have become heads of state, cabinet ministers, senior military officers, and leaders of business and industry. Their early associations in the United States have had a political value for our country which probably transcends the purely military importance of their training.

Another military contribution to foreign policy takes the form of advice rendered by military leaders to senior officials with regard to the capabilities and limitations of our armed forces and the role they might play in foreign policy. The Joint Chiefs of Staff are the primary source by virtue of their statutory responsibility to serve as the principal military advisers to the President, the National Security Council, and the Secretary of Defense. If the President eventually decides on the use of military force, the Joint Chiefs of Staff then act as a military staff for the Secretary of Defense, transmitting his orders to the combat forces and supervising the subsequent execution of the military mission.

Although there have always been critics in our country who charge undue military influence in the formulation and execution of foreign policy, to my knowledge no President, at least since World War II, has ever indicated concern on this score. On the contrary, following the Bay of Pigs fiasco, President Kennedy expressed disapproval of the lack of initiative shown by the Joint Chiefs of Staff in failing to express to him strongly enough their serious misgivings over the probable outcome of the Cuban landing. After emotion over the affair had subsided, on May 27, 1961, he called in person on the Joint Chiefs in the Pentagon to review the episode and to explain his concept of their advisory role. He indicated his regret that they had tried deliberately to limit their advice to answering only the specific questions directed to them and then only "from a military point of view"—an unduly narrow interpretation of their duty, as Kennedy saw it. In the President's view, his most difficult problems involved many factors—political, economic, and psychological, as well as military—and he needed advice applicable to their entirety, not to a part. He assured the Joint Chiefs that he did not regard them as narrow military specialists but as men of wide international experience who could help him in evaluating the broad context of many situations, particularly those requiring a combined input from many sources within government. To give his opinion lasting official status, this historic statement of the advisory role of the Joint Chiefs was incorporated in a National Security Memorandum, which was continued in effect throughout the Johnson administration and, I was informed, was revalidated by President Nixon.

As for the role of the armed forces in domestic policy, we should welcome whatever contribution they can make without dereliction of their primary tasks abroad and without improper intervention in domestic matters where most citizens would feel they do not belong.

To begin with, they should continue to perform their historic role as a military reserve behind the civil forces of law and order, available to assist the President in the discharge of his oath "to preserve, protect, and defend the Constitution" and to "insure the domestic tranquillity." The armed forces have performed these duties in situations as widely different as the defense of the Union in the Civil War and their occasional enforcement of school desegregation laws during the last two decades. Involvement in domestic conflicts is always unpleasant for men in uniform but it is an essential duty, one requiring meticulous training and special equipment if it is to be performed without unnecessary violence. If tragedies such as the Kent State affair are to be avoided, the armed forces will have to maintain, preferably in the National Guard, a few units with specialized training and equipment for dealing with such situations.

A second way in which the armed forces can serve domestic policy is by wise and effective use of the men, money, and materials made available to them. Rightly or wrongly, they have acquired a reputation for excessive budget requests, wastefulness in management, inefficient contracting methods, and apparent disregard for the taxpayer's dollar—an impression they can erase only by convincing evidence of a contrary behavior. A priority objective of the Pentagon should be to generate maximum military power from its resources and to use the end product with cost-conscious care and economy. I can suggest a few specific actions to this end for inclusion in the national security program.

At a time like the present, there is strong reason for the armed forces to review the role and missions of the military services—i.e., the Army, Navy, Air Force, and Marines—to see whether their current formulation, dating from shortly after World War II, remains valid for the coming era. In the passage of time, many overlaps have developed in service missions and, in my opinion, some have become obsolete or outmoded as a result of changes in strategy, tactics, and weaponry. Over the years, the intercontinental missile has replaced the long-range bomber as the primary delivery vehicle of strategic weapons. Our missile delivery systems have become so numerous that our strategic forces can now dispense with the reinforcement offered by carrier-based aircraft. The carriers can turn their attention to air support for ground forces and to antisubmarine operations, a form of warfare expanding in importance in proportion to the growth of the Soviet submarine fleet and American dependence on overseas markets and raw materials.

Even with this modified mission, the future of the large carrier is uncertain—at least in terms of numbers. Congress and elements in the Navy are pressing for nuclear propulsion for all new carriers and many smaller ships as well, an expensive improvement which will raise the cost of a large carrier to a billion dollars or more. This trend toward a nuclear-powered Navy is likely to be restrained not only by the cost but also by the undeniable need for a greater number of small, fast craft to patrol the sea lanes in which we have a growing national interest.

Another weapon system with an uncertain future is the land-based strategic missile force of the Air Force, which is becoming increasingly vulnerable to surprise attack by the large missiles of increasing accuracy which the Soviets are building. There is a growing feeling in many quarters in favor of phasing out land-based missiles and replacing them with submarine-launched missiles, if indeed any replacement is necessary.

The prime justification in the past for three heavy Marine divisions has been their use in large-scale amphibious operations, a relatively unlikely form of warfare in the emerging environment. The October 1973 campaign in the Mideast demonstrated the growing vulnerability of tanks and tactical aircraft to "smart" guided missiles, a development raising questions regarding the future utility of the Army's armored divisions and Air Force tactical aircraft over a modern battlefield. Meantime, our mobilization plans are still predicated largely on the needs for fighting a prolonged, conventional war in defense of NATO, an assumption costly in its force requirements and doubtful as to realism.

In their own interest, the armed forces will be obliged to control the skyrocketing prices of new equipment which result from a combination of inflation and the increasing complexity of modern weapons and equipment. It takes only a few billion-dollar carriers and *Trident* submarines, multimillion-dollar aircraft, and million-dollar tanks to absorb all the new equipment funds that the services are likely to receive in the hard times ahead.

Funds available for new equipment will be further curtailed by the personnel costs of the all-volunteer forces which now account for about 56 per cent of the 1975 Defense budget—in contrast to the 25 per cent thought to be allocated to personnel in the Soviet military budget. It is high time to obtain a professional opinion from the armed forces as to whether this is the best way to spend their money, and whether they can afford such payrolls and the implicit personnel retirement costs for the indefinite future.

The fact is that we are paying an extremely high price to avoid a peacetime draft, which most Americans following World War II had learned to accept with comparatively little complaint, by the adoption of a volunteer system of dubious reliability in time of war. It was the Vietnam war and the long casualty lists that generated most of the opposition to the draft and the demand for its abolition. Now we have a volunteer system which will work at an exorbitant cost while there is no shooting war in progress but which will not produce the manpower necessary to replace heavy combat casualties in wartime. When war comes, some change in the system will be essential to keep our forces manned for action.

After nearly three years of experience with the volunteer system, it is not unreasonable to ask the armed forces to report on the progress achieved, not merely in terms of the improved educational level of recruits, the reduction of the AWOL rate, or the numbers of re-enlistments, but with regard to more fundamental matters. Are volunteers providing us with combat-effective units of higher quality than those under the old mixed system of conscription and volunteering? Are we creating a mercenary military establishment formed largely of the poor, uneducated, and colored which may eventually become isolated from civil society and a political danger to the nation? Does it have the *esprit de corps* which holds men together in times of danger and hardship or do these men have the nine-to-five attitude of a hired man with little interest in his job and no feeling of kinship for his comrades? These are matters of national interest which deserve an answer as soon as the facts are available to support reliable conclusions.

As to the quality and reliability of this force in war or in serious civil disturbances, we cannot judge with finality until the contingency arises. If, for example, minority elements in the ranks were allowed to polarize along ethnic lines, as they frequently do in civil life, and if they should develop into factions aligned against one another in accordance with the political and social issues of the day, such divisions would create a pernicious disunity destructive of morale, discipline, and reliability. It would be equally disastrous to allow any form of unionization in the armed forces, an intolerable proposal recurrently advanced. Men under arms cannot have divided loyalties—they must be true to their commander, their comrades, and the mission of their unit; their personal interests must be absorbed into those of the military team of which they are members. Such attitudes and habits are quite different from the accepted norms of the members of a civilian community. But the latter are not leading a life of danger in which the failure of one individual may bring disaster to the group and failure to their common mission. A majority of the justices of the present Supreme Court recently expressed well this need to differentiate between the requirements of civilian and military life:

> To prepare for and perform its vital role (readiness for war), the military must insist upon a respect for duty and a discipline without counterpart in civilian life. The laws and traditions governing that discipline have a long history; but they are founded on unique military exigencies as powerful now as in the past. Their contemporary vitality repeatedly has been recognized by Congress.*

Such considerations emphasize the fallacy of the proposition that the life of the military should be made as similar as possible to that of civilians. It is a primary task of military training to prepare recruits for the transition from the ways of peace to those of the battlefield, and failure to do so would diminish their chance to survive and to carry out their tasks.

The armed forces have an opportunity to support domestic policy in other ways not directly related to their war-making mission—for

Schlesinger v. Councilman (February 2, 1975).

example, by demonstrating success in dealing with social problems such as drugs, liquor, and racial issues. After all, the strongest proof of the value of military service to the individual is evidence of improved quality in the men returning to civil life. Private citizens are in a position to verify by personal observation whether the improvement is a fact and thus to gain some insight into the true state of the military service on the inside.

The armed forces have an occasional opportunity to demonstrate civic responsibility through participation in nonmilitary activities such as disaster relief and programs for environmental and urban improvement. They have many assets applicable to such purposes— organization, trained manpower, and experience in construction, telecommunications, public health, transportation, and flood control. Abroad they have had a long record of performance in repairing the devastation caused by wars in which they have taken part, often learning by direct participation that it is more difficult to rebuild than to destroy a country. They engaged in the rehabilitation of the Axis nations after World War II and later in both South Korea and South Vietnam they conducted civic action programs in cooperation with the inhabitants which resulted in the construction of thousands of homes, schools, hospitals, churches, bridges, and market places.

Within the United States it has been comparatively rare for the armed forces to engage in such work on any scale. For one thing, labor unions are always worried that troop labor may take jobs away from them. For another, military commanders have feared a diversion from essential military tasks if the troops became unduly engaged in these nonmilitary activities. One major involvement did occur in the early 1930s at the height of the Great Depression, when the government called upon the armed forces to assist in the organization of the Civilian Conservation Corps (CCC), designed to employ jobless youths in flood control, countererosion, and reforestation. The job of the Army was to organize and administer the camps while representatives of the Department of the Interior usually supervised the work of the enrollees.

Should it ever be desirable, the armed forces could repeat or expand their performance in the CCC. There is often discussion of the advantages of some form of national service on a voluntary or compulsory basis which might provide useful work for the unemployed, as in the case of the CCC, serve as a physical or vocational training school, and possibly provide an alternative for military service. If conducted in the right way by the right people, national service could produce many desirable results—wholesome outdoor work for young city dwellers, early experience in living and working with people of differing backgrounds and origins, a resultant moderation of class and ethnic bias, and the eventual formation of better citizens from all participants.

Thus far we have discussed some of the ways in which the armed forces might support domestic policy. I would mention one activity from which we should want them to abstain—involvement in partisan politics either as individuals or as an institution. When a man dons the uniform, he assumes certain obligations and accepts certain restrictions on his freedom of action not required of civilians. Some limit, to varying degrees, the rights guaranteed the rest of us by the First, Fifth and Sixth amendments. In my own case, during nearly two decades of military service prior to World War II, I had only one legal opportunity to vote for a President. At all other times, I was debarred either by my inability to meet state residence requirements while living on a military reservation or by state laws, not uncommon at the time, excluding members of the armed forces from voting, often along with felons and imbeciles.

Since World War II, the removal of state restrictions on military voting and the extensive use of the absentee ballot for men serving outside their state of legal residence have removed the military from the ranks of the disenfranchised. But while this is commendable progress, it should not encourage the politicization of the armed forces. I stress this point because, in the domestic turmoil of the Vietnam war period, radical elements often tried and sometimes succeeded in infiltrating military posts with political propaganda and inducing soldiers to join in political demonstrations against the policies of the President, their Commander in Chief. Oddly, I noted few cries of public indignation and concern over these efforts, puny though they were, to detach men in uniform from their pledged loyalties.

What political activities are permissible for the man in uniform? I would say that he should certainly exercise his right to vote, and, to do so intelligently, he should have an understanding of the issues and the merits of the candidates. Beyond that, there is little he can do that will not bring divisive political issues into barracks or expose the armed forces to the charge of politicking for or against the government in office. Civilian elements seeking to involve the armed forces in politics are inviting the Man on Horseback, who, though often feared, has never appeared in American history.

For the benefit of national security policy planners seeking guidance, let me summarize the most important demands which should placed upon the military component of the national security program. We are agreed, I hope, that the armed forces should always give primary weight to their task of preventing war or waging war successfully. For this task they must maintain impressive strategic nuclear forces capable of deterring and neutralizing those of the USSR and conventional forces able to deal selectively with lesser military threats.

The armed forces should contribute to the support of foreign and domestic policy, utilizing their resources efficiently and responsibly whether engaged in military or civil tasks. Under all circumstances, quality must be the prime characteristic of these forces—quality always taking precedence over numbers. If budget costs or a shortage of qualified volunteers requires a reduction in numbers below the strength required by current missions, it becomes the duty of military leaders to seek a reduction in missions rather than to accept substandard manpower. Further, we citizens want to feel confidence and pride in our fighting men, a possibility only if they are visibly proud of their uniform, their profession, and themselves.

VI

The Requirements of Strategic Deterrence

The first task falling to the architects of the military component of a new national security policy will be to design an impressive strategic retaliatory force (SRF) capable of deterring any Soviet resort to strategic warfare and of neutralizing any effort by Moscow to use strategic power for political leverage or intimidation. For our purposes, strategic forces are those consisting of bombers, land-based missiles of intercontinental range, and submarine-launched missiles of the *Polaris-Poseidon* type, the targets of which are usually the war-sustaining resources of an enemy homeland—its government centers, cities, industry, military forces, and installations. Military targets are usually relatively small and often include "hard" elements protected by steel, concrete, or excavated shelters which require for their destruction warheads of either great accuracy, high yield, or both. Urban-industrial targets, on the contrary, are usually "soft"— i.e., unprotected and extending over wide areas—and thus may be destroyed by weapons of lesser accuracy or yield.

To meet the specifications we have laid down for the SRF, our security planners must first agree on what should be meant by deterrence. As I would define it, *deterrence* describes a psychological condition of Soviet leaders which inhibits any resort to strategic weapons against the United States or its allies. We would expect this condition to arise if they had a conviction approaching certainty that a strategic attack upon us or any target embodying a vital American interest would invoke a counterattack in kind which would inflict intolerable damage in spite of anything they could do to prevent it. If the Soviet leaders are rational men who understand, as we assume they do, the destructive effects of strategic weapons and American ability to produce these effects, it seems reasonable to believe that they will reach the desired frame of mind if convinced on at least two points.

The first would be the destructiveness and indestructibility of the American strategic forces—a conviction that, even after a surprise attack, there would be enough accurate and reliable weapons remaining for us to inflict such incapacitating damage as to make this course of action clearly unremunerative. The second point would be an assurance that the American President, secure from destruction himself, would issue the necessary orders to retaliate and that these orders would be transmitted over protected communications to weapons commanders who would carry them out. So understood, deterrence depends essentially on an assured destructive capability, a reliable, protected communications net, and a strong President unlikely to flinch from his responsibility.

It is difficult to imagine the pressure which would bear upon a President in such a case. Truman's decision to use the first nuclear weapons against Japan would not be comparable—nothing in history has been. A President's first concern would likely be the consequences of his action on his own people. Will enough survive to claim a "victory"even if his side ends with more survivors than the "vanquished"? Will these survivors hold the President responsible for their plight—assuming he himself survives? How would other countries treat his stricken nation—perhaps like wolves leaping on a wounded leader of the pack? Would Mexican neighbors swarm across the Rio Grande to regain the Southwest from the Yanqui invaders of another century? His Soviet counterpart in Moscow might have similar thoughts about the actions of the European satellites at such a time. Would they rise to give the *coup de grâce* to a feared oppressor *in extremis?* Would Mao's armies in the East move to wrest old

Chinese territories from Soviet hands? Both sides might properly fear an outraged international community endangered by their reckless resort to strategic arms.

Such reflections emphasize the importance of the character and will of the President as a factor adding to the deterrent effect of our weapons. Since the attitude of a President will be strongly influenced by that of the people whom he represents, national character also participates in the effectiveness and stability of deterrence.

In addition to the moral qualities of the President and the nation, there are a number of other factors which may stabilize or undermine deterrence. Take, for example, the indestructibility conferred on the opposing forces by numbers, concealment, hardening, or mobility. To the extent that they both enjoy these advantages it will be correspondingly difficult for one side to hope to destroy the weapons of the other by a surprise attack. Also, if both sides have unprotected cities, the "balance of terror" will tend to remain stable. For the present, urban vulnerability is deliberately accepted by both sides under the terms of the SALT I agreement, which limits the antiballistic missile defense of cities to Moscow and Washington—a protection that Congress has thus far denied the American capital, the focal control point of our strategic weapons system.

On the other hand, the balance may be destabilized by actions suggesting an intention to develop a first-strike capability—for example, a sharp increase in numbers of weapons or some technological breakthrough promising a decisive advantage to one side. On this score there has been criticism of our MIRV (multiple independently targeted re-entry vehicle) program, which packages into a single warhead a number of relatively small warheads which can be guided individually to different targets. By this device we obtain many more small warheads in place of fewer large ones and thus increase the numbers of targets that can be attacked while reducing unnecessary damage due to overkill. Similar criticism has been raised against efforts to increase the accuracy of our missiles on the ground that accuracy facilitates their use against military targets like ICBM silos and thus suggests a first-strike intention.

Another destabilizing factor would be the existence of exposed targets inviting attack, such as keypoints of the military communications system, unprotected strategic bombers concentrated on airfields, or ICBMs in soft or in sufficiently unprotected silos. During the Cuba missile crisis in 1962, President Kennedy became so concerned about a possible Soviet attack on soft U.S. missiles deployed in Turkey that he had them removed after the crisis was over.

So much for the anatomy of strategic deterrence. As we proceed with the design of a strategic retaliatory force, we must keep in mind those factors which maximize and stabilize deterrence and thus provide guidance as to its optimum size and composition.

One day in 1956, Secretary of Defense Wilson asked me as Army Chief of Staff what I thought was the most difficult issue before the Joint Chiefs of Staff at that time. I answered without hesitation, "How much is enough in strategic nuclear weapons?" The issue remains open today.

Immediately following World War II this was not a burning question because we had so little fissionable material and so few weapons. The objective of the military was simply to add as many weapons each year to the limited stockpile as technology and production would permit. This situation changed, however, with the launching of *Sputnik I* in 1957, an event that aroused apprehension over a possible Soviet superiority in rocketry and thereby greatly stimulated the American missile programs and the output of nuclear warheads. Soon President Kennedy and, shortly afterward, President Johnson were faced with answering the question: "How much is enough?"

To my knowledge, the first formula proposed for sufficiency was a strategic force that could assure the destruction of a large percentage of the population and industrial capacity of the USSR even after absorbing a massive first strike. The actual percentages assumed varied from time to time but, translated into human and economic losses, any percentage used would have amounted to a total national disaster surpassing anything in all historical experience. The proposed concentration of attack on urban-industrial targets resulted from two considerations. In the absence of the high-quality photography now available, we lacked precise information on most military targets, particularly missile sites. Also, since we always assumed that the Soviets would strike first, our side would never be sure of the location of the bombers and missiles that had not been expended in the first strike. However, in the course of the Johnson administration, senior officials occasionally referred rather vaguely to the possible need for striking some counterforce—i.e., military—targets as well as urban areas. Such targeting was entirely possible by procedures existing at the time.

The Nixon administration, seeking something better than or at least different from the "assured destruction" formula, first adopted "strategic sufficiency" as its goal. The latter was defined as the ability in a second strike to inflict roughly as much population and industrial damage on the USSR as we had already suffered in the first strike. This would have been very difficult to do because of the attrition of our forces to be expected in the first strike and the greater concentration of the American population in urban areas than the Russian. Thus, in effect, the modified formula set a higher standard than "assured destruction."

President Nixon did not long remain satisfied with "strategic sufficiency" because, in case of a limited strategic attack, he felt it left him no option other than doing nothing or responding with a massive attack on Soviet cities. The corrective was yet another formula of adequacy—"essential equivalence." This phrase described a situation in which United States strategic forces are essentially equal to the Soviet forces in all important aspects and organized to permit a limited strategic response to a limited strategic attack while retaining an invulnerable reserve capable of reaching the standard of "strategic sufficiency" previously defined. To afford the President this option, the armed forces were directed to give additional flexibility to targeting procedures, to increase the accuracy of weapons and, if necessary, their yields, in order to permit engaging hard and soft military targets with minimum damage outside the immediate target area.

As a final element of the new formula, Secretary of Defense Schlesinger stressed the importance of *perceived* essential equivalence—

that is, friend and foe, official and private citizen, expert and layman must be able to perceive that, taking into account all pertinent factors, our forces were at least as formidable as those of our rival.

The implications of perceived essential equivalence so interpreted have aroused interest and controversy at home and abroad. There are really two issues involved: the feasibility or desirability of waging limited strategic war under certain circumstances and the practicability of achieving perceived equivalence before such a mixed gallery of perceivers.

As to the first point, it is certainly conceivable that a particularly bold or reckless head of state, contemptuous of a timid adversary despite his possession of strategic weapons, might attempt to intimidate the latter by threats or by actually attacking a limited number of targets with strategic weapons either to reduce the retaliatory power of the victim or merely to warn him of greater damage if he did not capitulate. With his disdain for French and British leadership at the start of World War II, Hitler, given nuclear weapons, would have been capable of such a gambit in order to secure a prompt surrender in the West. Even if the leadership of a country so threatened refused to crumple, the detonation of a few nuclear weapons in the homeland might be sufficient to create uncontrollable panic and chaos, which would lead to national disintegration and eventual surrender. If, in the 1930s, an Orson Welles broadcast describing a fictional landing of Martians on earth was sufficient to terrify thousands of Americans, what would happen today if we suddenly learned that an enemy missile had just exploded, say, near a Minuteman silo in Wyoming or the Dakotas?

However, it would not be easy for an aggressor to choose so venturesome a course regardless of his confidence in his evaluation of a weak opponent. The latter might have a Joan of Arc somewhere in his entourage capable of instilling in him the necessary resolve to push the button firing his retaliatory weapons in a crippling counterblow. Both leaders in such a crisis would have occasion to fear their own people, who would have good cause to resent the dangers to which they had been exposed and to hold their leaders to account.

It is quite possible that the latter would become prime candidates for Nuremberg justice without benefit of judge or jury.

The initiator of a limited exchange would have another cause for concern. Suppose that, when he gave the order to fire, the missiles failed to lift off, aborted in flight, missed the target, or, worse, hit the wrong target? Instead of bursting in the air as intended, they might detonate on impact, thereby raising vast clouds of nuclear debris to drift eastward in the prevailing winds and gradually deposit their lethal contents over thousands of square miles of territory, perhaps in a neighboring country. Then he would be not only an international criminal, but a ridiculous bungler as well. Since no nation has ever completely tested a strategic missile system from launch to warhead detonation on target, these are not farfetched possibilities. It would be miraculous if there were no serious "bugs" in these complex weapons when first used such as have always plagued new and intricate devices. So let the first user beware!

As between the two great nuclear powers, one would think that the Soviets would be much more tempted to try the limited gambit than the United States. They would have some grounds to hope that U.S. leaders would be loath to retaliate, either from humanitarian considerations, fear of disavowal by their own people, or lack of will. They would be aware of the physical exposure of the President and his advisors in Washington and the vulnerability to attack of many centers of the command and control system, knowledge that might father the hope of paralyzing our response by a few well-placed weapons, most likely on Washington.

On the other side of the argument, the Soviets must always consider China's reaction if they become involved in even a limited nuclear exchange with the United States. Also, they may lack confidence in the accuracy of their weapons, a suspicion encouraged by the numbers and the large size of many of their warheads. Finally, a limited use of strategic weapons implies a certain finesse in the use of violence inconsistent with the style of the Soviet military, who have always tended to seek victory through massive concentrations of men and firepower with utter disregard for military or civilian losses.

But they are also inclined to be cautious about taking unnecessary risks. Hence, I am inclined to believe that the Politburo would much prefer to await the collapse of capitalist America and its allies from economic and political forces already at work than to run the risks of playing dangerous games with Promethean fire.

Certainly there is nothing of advantage in the nature of this game which would incline United States leaders to initiate it. However, it is always possible that the United States might sometime be faced with the need to respond to a limited attack. Given the prospect of considerable further proliferation of nuclear weapons, the situation might arise without Soviet involvement as the result of a reckless or irrational act of some new possessor of nuclear weapons. Finally, an indicated readiness to make a limited strategic response short of an attack on cities to a major Soviet provocation might reassure allies dependent on the American nuclear umbrella. Hence, taking all factors into account, I have rather reluctantly accepted the need for earmarking a small number of strategic weapons for use in limited reprisals in case this need should arise.

I would hope that we could make this provision without excessive additional costs. But if a limited exchange has any real possibility, there would be a case for renewed expenditures on civil defense, the building of more shelters for the civil population, and updated plans for the emergency evacuation of cities. Since the damage to be expected will be severe but localized, there may also be justification for protected stock piles of supplies and equipment for the purposes of disaster relief. In short, once we accept limited strategic warfare as feasible and probable—something which I strongly doubt—we open up a long list of costly additives to the security bill that we may be asked to pay, including even new strategic weapons of special design for this particular purpose. However, despite the superficial logic of their case, I would oppose the inclusion of these costly additives in the national security program.

The second issue raised by the concept of perceived essential equivalence is the requirement that the essential parity of our strategic strength with the Soviets' be clearly perceptible to friend and foe.

As I understand it, essential parity amounts to rough equality in numbers of weapons, throw weight, yield, accuracy, reliability, and so forth, although an advantage in some of these characteristics apparently may compensate for inferiority in others. In defending the SALT II agreements in Vladivostok, administration officials have pointed out that while the USSR for the present has more missiles, greater missile throw weight, and higher warhead yields, the United States has more warheads due to MIRV, more bombers, and greater missile accuracy. One assumes that in their view this situation meets the requirements of perceived essential equivalence.

Secretary Schlesinger has explained the importance of the perceptibility of equivalence or better as being "for symbolic purposes in large part because the strategic forces have come to be seen by many —however regrettably—as the status and stature of a major power." Another reason, in his view, was that "the lack of equality can become a source of serious diplomatic and military miscalculation," and thus may cause allies to question our dependability and even arouse doubts among ourselves as to the government's ability to protect us and the national interests. On the other hand, a sense of superiority —or at least parity—with the Soviets would tend to strengthen the backbone of American leaders in a critical confrontation.

All of these arguments have a certain validity but they raise a number of troubling questions. Who must perceive what and how? The "who" certainly includes policy makers in the United States, the USSR, and allied countries, but in official statements there are implications that the average man in the street should also perceive this vision. To be seen and understood by such a numerous and heterogeneous audience, the components of equivalence must be within the range of perception and understanding not merely of experts but also of nontechnical laymen. It is well to remind ourselves that the latter category includes most heads of state, senior government officials, and legislators who are normally not versed in the arcane technology of the nuclear specialists.

What must such lay observers be able to perceive in order to form the desired conviction that U.S. strategic forces are at least as strong as those of the Soviets? Somehow they must receive convincing evidence of the relative merit of the two forces as measured by the key characteristics of quality noted above. But here we encounter serious obstacles. How do we get access to equally reliable data on the rival forces to serve as a basis for comparison? The USSR never officially reveals significant data on their weapons. Even in the SALT discussions held under the protection of tight official secrecy, the Soviet representatives never inform their American counterparts of the number or characteristics of their own strategic weapons—they simply accept without confirmation or denial the data used by American officials which are provided by American intelligence sources. In contrast, our side does submit selected official data on our forces to the Soviet representatives—we could hardly withhold all information since so much is routinely released to the news media in accordance with the prevailing mode of governmental openness. Thus, the earnest perceiver seeking to compare forces must depend on an interested party, the United States, for all information bearing on both sides which, as it affects the Soviet forces, will be tainted by whatever errors there are in American intelligence reports.

Inevitably, U.S. intelligence on Soviet strategic forces has its limitations and imperfections. Satellite photography can produce detailed pictures of such things as ICBM silos and launch facilities, missile-carrying submarines, long-range bombers, and storage sites presumably containing nuclear warheads. In Moscow parades, observers may see actual missiles on transporters but usually only obsolescent types. American experts can interpret the technical data obtainable and reach rough estimates on such matters as missile ranges, accuracy, dimensions, and warhead characteristics. But no one has ever seen enough actual missiles or warheads to permit an accurate estimate of the size and quality of the Soviet arsenal. The only perception of Soviet strength available to an observer with access to American sources is an image derived from interpretations of photographs and other technological data associated with the nuclear weapons which constitute the core of Soviet strategic strength—truly an image seen "as through a glass, darkly." A perverse skeptic might even wonder whether all this imagery might not be a clever Soviet contrivance with mirrors to lead Americans into error and thereby cause them to acquire an exaggerated impression of Soviet strength. After all, the Soviets have never seriously challenged the American estimates of their forces, whereas they challenge almost everything else. Their silence suggests that they are not dissatisfied with our figures.

The evidence available to the lay perceiver is not only indirect and opaque but is not likely to mean much to him. It takes something of an expert to draw meaningful conclusions from data regarding missile guidance systems, circular probable errors, launch and in-flight vulnerabilities, nuclear environmental phenomena, and warhead configurations. Even the expert would have trouble establishing the relative merits of missile A over missile B if A were superior to B in some important characteristics and inferior in others. About the only data that could convey a perception of strength or weakness to the average layman would be those regarding the numbers of weapons and their destructive capabilities. Numbers are likely to be particularly convincing since we have long been accustomed to measuring military strength in terms of numbers of divisions, ships, airplanes, and men under arms.

But, unfortunately, if we wish to take numbers of strategic weapons as a primary criterion of relative strength, we must first decide what numbers to compare. Before the development of MIRVs, we could compare missile launchers under the limitations previously described and feel safe to assume that every missile launcher had one missile which had one warhead of an approximate weight and yield (estimated, of course, in the case of Soviet weapons). Thus, prior to MIRVs the number of launch sites counted on photos were considered equal to the number of missiles available which, in turn, equated to the number of warheads which represented destructive capacity, the ultimate measure of strategic strength.

Now that each long-range missile may carry a number of warheads, the warhead count is not so simple—indeed, for Soviet missiles, it cannot be calculated with a high degree of accuracy by any means available to us. For that reason, in undertaking to limit the numbers of strategic weapons in the SALT II talks in Vladivostok, it was necessary to specify two figures: 2,400, the maximum permitted number of delivery vehicles, and 1,320, the number of delivery vehicles within the 2,400 that might carry multiple warheads. But since there was no limit set on the number of warheads permitted within the 1,320, no one seeking evidence of equivalence could ascertain the number of warheads that each side might have under the agreement at any particular time. Thus, numbers of missiles or warheads turn out to be an unsatisfactory measure of relative strength.

Perhaps, then, we might use relative destructive strength of weapons as our primary criterion since destructiveness may be expressed in a manner easily understood and highly impressive. One graphic way is to state the explosive power of a megaton weapon as being so many times the power of the Hiroshima bomb. Most of us have seen pictures of that devastated Japanese city and can form some vague concept of the awful destructiveness of the megatonnage of larger weapons.

But again we run into difficulties if we take megatonnage or throw weight as a prime measure of the destructive effectiveness of weapons. The fact is that a weapon of larger megatonnage is not necessarily more effective under all conditions than a smaller one. There are two factors which vitiate such an assumption: accuracy and overkill. Scientists point out that a multimegaton weapon with a probable error of one-half mile may be less effective in destroying a hard target than a one-megaton weapon with a probable error of one-sixth mile. Thus accuracy improvement under certain conditions is much more advantageous than an increase in numbers or in megatonnage of weapons. But, as we have noted, accuracy is not a quality that a layman can perceive for himself.

Overkill is a condition resulting from the fact that much of the explosive effect of a large nuclear airburst is concentrated on the ground immediately beneath the fireball where everything is destroyed many times over with a needless expenditure of energy. Overkill may also be used to denote the excessive potential for destruction represented by the weapons in the present national arsenal which, in theory at least, could destroy every conceivable target system we might wish to strike and have an excess left over. When nuclear weapons were first being developed, our military leaders, recognizing the fact of overkill, assumed that we would eventually reach a finite quantity of nuclear material which, reworked as needed to meet recurring changes in weapon design, would be sufficient for all future needs. Somewhere along the decades that thought was lost, so now we appear obsessed with a need for constantly increasing numbers of weapons and deliverable megatonnage largely, I am afraid, to keep up with the Soviet Joneses.

By this time, we are obliged to conclude that neither numbers, accuracy, throw weight, nor megatonnage is a reliable, convincing, or perceptible measure of comparative strategic strength. Is there any other better alternative to serve our purpose?

Because of the difficulties noted above, I doubt that we can ever make a convincing, direct comparison of the two strategic forces. Could we circumvent the difficulty by comparing our own destructive capability with that required to destroy the target systems that we might wish to attack and thereby determine how much destruction is enough so far as needs are concerned? If we can express the destructiveness of our entire strategic arsenal in a simple but graphic manner that takes overkill into account, we might hope that evidence of the vastness of our strength would to a large extent moot the issue of Soviet strength. Our case could be particularly strong if we could state that our estimated destructive capacity assumed very little help from bombers penetrating Soviet air defenses and the loss of most of our ICBMs by a Soviet first strike. If, under those conditions, our arsenal could still destroy everything we might need to destroy, and the Soviets and all other interested parties knew it, our offensive strategic strength should leave nothing to be desired.

As a means for expressing U.S. destructive capabilities, I would suggest adopting two notional units of measurement, one a unit of urban destruction (UUD), the other a unit of military destruction (UMD). The first would be a combination of warheads capable of achieving a desired level of destruction with minimum overkill in a typical city area, say, five miles square, with population density, buildings, and industrial establishments comparable to those in major Soviet cities. The UMD would be an analogous warhead combination required for the destruction of a military area, say, two miles square, containing typical military installations, both hard and soft, such as command posts, barracks, an airfield, nuclear storage facilities, or missile launch sites. Experts in weapons effects could tell us how many of our warheads in what combination of sizes would be theoretically necessary to effect such destruction with minimum overkill.

Using these units, our leaders could then define the capability of our strategic arsenal in square miles of urban-industrial area and the number of military areas that the weapons could destroy. This total could then be compared with the lesser area containing the actual targets of an "assured destruction" reprisal attack. In this way, there would be no direct mention of numbers, precision, reliability, megatonnage, or invulnerability, although our experts would have taken all of these factors into account in their computations. Under present and foreseeable conditions, I would expect the results to indicate such an excess in destructive capability as to silence any serious demand to acquire more weapons, almost regardless of what the Soviets may do.

The public statement of our strategic potential could be expressed in the following terms: Assuming the destruction of most of our ICBM and strategic bomber forces by a Soviet first strike, the remaining strategic retaliatory forces of the United States would be able to destroy with a probability approaching 100 per cent, X number of Soviet cities containing 20 to 30 per cent of the Soviet population and 40 to 50 per cent of their industrial capacity and Y number of military complexes containing the principal headquarters, communication centers, and war-sustaining military facilities of the USSR. This destruction could be accomplished without resort to deliberate ground bursts of warheads while retaining a reserve capability of repeating the retaliation Z times.

To convert this formula from a statement of potential to one of sufficiency it would be necessary for the President to give values to X, Y, and Z. For example, he might decide that in his judgment our strategic forces would be sufficient if, under the assumptions, they could destroy about one hundred cities and perhaps thirty military complexes while retaining a reserve capable of repeating the retaliation once. Additional weapons in the arsenal beyond those needed for this level of strength would be available for bargaining force reductions with the Soviets. Through this procedure, we might hope to escape the thrall of numbers and mitigate the present possibility of self-intimidation by a delusive perception of an unreal danger.

Before closing this discussion, we must remind ourselves that we have omitted any consideration of the will of opposing leaderships as an element of perceived essential equivalence; yet it is certainly a preponderant factor. Strategic strength is merely a part of the military contribution to overall national posture to which the character of leaders and people makes major contributions. All parts of national power are interdependent, so that the strength of one does not necessarily compensate for the weakness of another. The United States might conceivably be vastly superior to the Soviet Union in strategic forces, as it was until recent times, and still succumb from inadequate government, internal disunity, or a failing economy, without the laying-on of an enemy hand. Or we might excel the Soviets in all forms of power except in numbers of strategic weapons and surrender to a self-created illusion of weakness. We might even enjoy perceived essential equivalence as measured by any of the means discussed and still invite strategic intimidation or attack if our leaders appeared too weak to lead or our people too divided to follow. Material strength, perceived or covert, is of little avail if the spirit fails.

VII

The Requirements for Conventional Forces

If we found it difficult to arrive at a formula for sufficiency for the strategic retaliatory force, it will prove no easier for the conventional forces* although the difficulties will be of a different order. In the case of the strategic forces, we had at least the advantage of knowing the probable enemy against whom to prepare and the likely target system against which to measure the destructive capabilities of our forces. No such constants are present to guide security planners in setting standards of sufficiency for conventional forces.

Over the years there have been many attempts to find a convincing way to establish a case for conventional forces of a certain size and composition in accordance with some accepted standard of sufficiency. Since World War II, their case has usually been based on the need to fulfill our NATO commitment and concurrently to be able to do something else somewhere else. In practice, the NATO commitment has come to mean the retention in Europe of a permanent force of about five divisions (four-and-one-third divisions at present) with appropriate supporting air and logistic forces. In addition, a variable number of Regular and Reserve† divisions in the United

---

*Also known as *general purpose forces*—the Pentagon term.

†*Reserve* (with a capital *R*) refers to military units and personnel outside the permanent military establishment—e.g., the Army National Guard.

States have been earmarked for a prompt reinforcement of NATO in an emergency.

The ability to do "something else somewhere else" simultaneously has sometimes been defined as a capacity merely to suppress some relatively insignificant brush fire, but at other times, the task has been expanded to mean an ability to deal with a brush fire plus a sizable conflict of the order of the Korean War. These variants have often been referred to as a *one-and-one-half* or a *two-and-one-half war capability*. In reality, these terms have been misleading by suggesting to the public that the Department of Defense sought a permanent military establishment able to wage several wars at a time. Actually the Pentagon never harbored such grandiose ideas and has never sought funds for forces of the magnitude implied. Likewise, Defense has never sought "essential equivalence" of conventional forces with those of the Soviets, in contradiction with the current position of the Department regarding strategic forces. One may ask why, if it is intolerable to accept inferiority in the strategic field, we do not require superiority or at least equivalence in conventional forces.

The obvious answer is that the United States' need for conventional forces is likely to be quite different from that of the Soviets—or of any other foreign nation, for that matter. Under present world conditions, the Soviets must maintain strong forces along the Sino-Soviet frontier and in certain of the European satellites suspected of inclining to political deviationism. These forces are deployed along the boundary of what I would call the Soviet primary security zone which embraces the vital assets and resources of the USSR and the Warsaw Pact. They are virtually immobilized in place by the permanence and importance of their mission.

On the other hand, the primary security zone of the United States does not require this kind of close-in perimeter defense. Our primary security zone encompasses the concentration of national valuables and interests found in greatest density in North America and the Caribbean area with a lesser distribution throughout the rest of the Western Hemisphere as far south as about the Tropic of Capricorn. It includes the coastal waters and sea approaches of the hemisphere and the maritime lines of communication linking the zone to our overseas military bases, our principal trade partners, and extrahemispheric sources of important raw materials. With a powerful Navy covering the sea approaches, we have no need for strong ground forces constantly on guard along our land frontiers. We do require fixed forces for our garrisons in NATO, the Western Pacific, Panama, and Alaska, but they do not compare with the Soviet forces protecting their extensive eastern and western borders.

If we do not require "essential equivalence" with the USSR because of the asymmetry of conventional military tasks, how should our needs be expressed in terms of relative strength to our principal rival? I would contend that against any enemy we need conventional superiority, actual or potential, throughout our primary security zone which, as described above, constitutes a hemispheric island with maritime tentacles reaching to those overseas sources from which the homeland draws an increasing amount of political and economic support. If the United States is prudent, its leaders will be slow in undertaking political commitments which may require military support at any great distance from this primary zone. Just as Khrushchev found to his sorrow that the Caribbean was not the place to challenge the United States, it would be folly for us to become militarily involved alone with the Soviets in close proximity to their primary security zone. This is a part of the world in which I for one am prepared to concede them relative military superiority as a routine matter.

But between the two national security zones there is a vast intermediate no man's land in which many nations, including the United States and the USSR, have important interests. If an American statesman seeks to achieve his ends by persuasion or inducement in contending with an adversary outside our security zone, he must always be aware of the possibility that the situation may get out of hand and require the use of military force under disadvantageous conditions. If the Soviets were the adversary, the outcome of a resort to arms would depend on many factors: the character of the opposing leaders at the moment and the popular support they enjoyed at home; logistic factors determining the size and composition of the forces that could be assembled in time to affect the outcome; relative war-sustaining capacity of the adversaries measured in trained manpower, war industry, strategic transport, logistic facilities, and national endurance; the help that would be contributed by allies; and the possession of strategic weapons adequate to deter their use by the enemy. Conceptually, one might imagine the existence of a power isobar encompassing the globe where these aggregated factors have an equal value for both sides which could serve as a warning of the limit of the respective spheres of prudent intervention.

To illustrate the working of these factors, take a situation that is far from impossible—that of a military confrontation between the United States and the USSR in the Middle East as an outgrowth of renewed Arab-Israeli hostilities. The size of the forces brought to bear by each contestant would be controlled not so much by the size of the overall military establishment at home as by the forces which could be relieved from their peacetime duties, transported, and sustained in combat in the Middle East. In the end, it is likely that troop availability, strategic mobility, and logistic facilities would be the dominant military factors controlling the size of the forces.

In comparing relative logistic advantages, the United States would probably have an edge in global logistic experience derived from World War II, Korea, and Vietnam and in the quantity and quality of strategic sea and air transport, but would suffer from the disadvantage of distance from the United States and of dependence on uncertain allies for the use of port and airfield facilities. In view of the turbulent political situation in Portugal and of NATO opposition encountered in 1973 to United States action in replacing Israeli battle losses in equipment from American stocks in Europe, the availability of allied facilities in a confrontation with the USSR over Israel must be considered questionable.

Although the USSR would have the advantage of proximity, it would have an urgent need for continuous passage of naval vessels from the Black Sea to the Mediterranean, a thoroughfare controlled by the Turkish government. Otherwise, Soviet strategic transport to the combat area would be dependent largely on cargo aircraft overflying Turkey or Iran and landing on friendly Arab fields.

As for the quality of the armed forces, I would expect it to be high on both sides. Since logistic difficulties will limit the size of the forces introduced, both governments should be able to send only their best units. Similarly, I would credit both sides with an ability to sustain their forces adequately in combat provided the necessary logistic systems could be installed and kept functioning, possibly under enemy attack. Likewise, the strategic forces of the two sides should be adequate for mutual deterrence.

There remains the political factor represented by the national leadership and popular attitudes. In an appraisal of these matters of the spirit, logic is likely to be less useful than intuition, although past national behavior in somewhat analogous situations may provide a basis for estimate. In the case of American leadership, for reasons already discussed, I would not expect a President to act quickly and decisively in sending forces into combat in the Middle East or any place else. To avoid the danger of being called back by Congress under the War Powers Act, he would certainly prefer to have advance congressional approval and possibly a new conscription law to assure meeting manpower requirements. He would like to have assurance of permission from Portugal to land aircraft in the Azores; from Spain, Italy, and Greece for overflight authority and possibly the use of certain Mediterranean ports and airfields. He would hope that Turkey would agree to close the Straits to the vessels of belligerents. Most of all, he must evaluate the likely duration of popular support for a cause that many Americans would view as less than vital and exposed to serious risk of failure. Regardless of the size of the military establishment at home, he would be beset by serious and justified doubt as to his ability to establish and maintain United States superiority over the USSR long enough to attain the political objective, presumably the long-term viability of Israel as an independent state. With the ever-growing disparity of strength between the Arab states and Israel, that would be a very ambitious objective and one difficult, if not impossible, to attain and retain for an indefinite period.

One cannot be certain of the effect of political factors in the

USSR. However, it is fair to imagine that the men in the Kremlin would hesitate to violate the well-established and remunerative practice of keeping Soviet forces within their own security zone and leaving the fighting outside to proxies. This restraining factor might be reinforced by concern for Peking's reaction to Soviet military involvement and by the historical record that Soviet forces have done their best only when fighting in defense of Mother Russia.

The overall conclusion I would draw from this discussion of conventional military superiority or equivalence is that it is not a condition determinable by comparative tabulations of men under arms, numbers of divisions, and quantities of military equipment, although such statistics have their importance. Where, when, why, and how long are questions that must be considered before making a case for or against the possibility of military superiority at a given point and a final answer must include consideration of political, economic, and spiritual matters, as well as military ones. *Military superiority* is not an absolute term but one describing rival capabilities under specific conditions of time, place, and duration. To have validity it must take into account all forms of relevant national power.

Because of difficulties encountered in justifying specific numbers of conventional forces on the basis of a requirement for "NATO plus something" or for rough equality with Soviet forces, I would prefer to fall back on a commonplace analogy from everyday life—the need of a nation, like that of an individual, to buy insurance for protection against future uncertainties. Most of us pay considerable sums each year in insurance premiums to secure ourselves against the consequences of death, illness, or accidents and, as our insurables increase in number and value, we try to increase their insurance proportionately, even at the cost of pleasures and comforts in which we like to indulge. A similar approach would be possible and highly desirable in determining the size of the national military budget and the portion therein which can be allocated to conventional forces.

It would be a happy day if Congress and the general public would agree to regard national security in all its aspects as a form of insurance for which an annual premium must be paid, of a size related to the value of the assets protected. Although it is impossible to attach an accurate price tag to the valuables of a nation, particularly those intangibles like liberty, unity, and domestic tranquility, the Gross National Product as the annual output of the economy in goods and services provides a useful measure against which to compare expenditures for security purposes. Hence, I would propose setting aside each year an agreed percentage of the GNP to meet the military requirements of security in any normal year. Although in a specific year Congress could increase or decrease the percentage for cause, the establishment of this base line budget representing what we feel we should spend for military security would tend to stabilize military planning and dampen the wide fluctuations of the military budget which cause inefficiency in the management of the many multiyear defense programs.

Once the aggregate dollar figure of a specific military budget was established, Pentagon authorities could rather quickly estimate the funds necessary to maintain adequate strategic forces, and to defray the fixed costs of paying, training, housing, transporting, and administering the military establishment. The funds left over would constitute those available for conventional forces in that year and would represent what the country felt it could afford to pay for this particular form of military protection. Being what we could afford, this force would necessarily be sufficient since more would constitute extravagance, which by definition is excessive.

Such a procedure would not diminish the ability of Congress to supervise adequately the major military programs, particularly those involving the development and production of costly weapons systems. Congress has the right and duty not only to decide how much the country can afford for military purposes but also to determine in cooperation with the Executive the kind of security the armed forces should provide. These are the policy areas that deserve close attention and should constitute the chief issues for public discussion and congressional debate. If the services know the overall amount they will have to spend and the part thereof to be applied to major weapons systems both strategic and conventional, after making provision for fixed charges which cannot be altered, they will have little money left for reckless spending.

This may be the proper time to point out that dollars are not the sole restraint on the size of the armed forces. With the advent of the all-volunteer system, the ability of the services to recruit acceptable volunteers may also impose a ceiling. In 1975, under the conditions of economic recession, it was possible only by dint of herculean efforts to maintain 2.1 million men under arms, a number barely adequate to carry out the current missions assigned to the services. When good times return, it may prove impossible to maintain that strength without lowering the standards for recruit acceptance—the latter a course that should be resolutely rejected in favor of maintaining excellence in the ranks at all costs. But even if qualified recruits were plentiful, the services could hardly afford to enlist greater numbers because of their high pay scales. At the moment, about 57 per cent of the Defense budget goes to the pay of personnel, a figure which rises to about 70 per cent in the Army. Hence any increase in the Defense budget at this time should go for research and development, equipment, supplies, and maintenance rather than for more people.

While advocating an annual military budget based on a fixed percentage of the GNP, I have not ventured to suggest a specific figure. Obviously, this would be an important issue to be thrashed out in the Executive branch and then debated in Congress. For a number of reasons, my offhand opinion would be that a figure of about 8 per cent of the GNP would be justified at this time.

In fiscal year 1975, the corresponding figure was 5.9 per cent and the military component of the total federal budget amounted to 29 per cent. In contrast, at the start of our combat involvement in South Vietnam in 1965 the figures were something over 8 per cent of the GNP and nearly 45 per cent of the federal budget. Meanwhile, by 1975 American security and prestige have declined sharply below the level of 1964 and the nation confronts a turbulent future.

I have already made the point that we are suffering today from political and economic weakness at home, the enfeebled condition of our principal allies, and the tragic consequences of our defeat in Southeast Asia. While added military strength is not all that is needed to regain our former position as a respected great power, this is no time to appear deliberately to acquiesce in a diminished role in world affairs. As a reaffirmation of our determination to regain our former high estate and to defend our interests in the coming decade of troubles, an increased military budget would be a convincing action which all observers would understand.

Even after a determination of the funds and manpower available for the conventional forces, the Secretary of Defense and the Joint Chiefs of Staff would have to decide on the distribution of these resources among the overseas deployments, the central reserve, and naval forces for safeguarding important sea lanes and supporting overseas operations. To make this allocation it would first be necessary to reach agreement on several subsidiary issues—the proper size and location of the forces assigned to the defense of NATO, the missions of the forces of the central reserve, and the dimensions of the naval mission of safeguarding the sea lanes. The NATO issue is by far the most controversial.

In 1975 we had in Europe a force of four-and-one-third divisions and associated air units, roughly 300,000 military personnel and many thousands of military dependents. Furthermore, we had earmarked in the central reserve at home several additional divisions and air units as ready reinforcements to send to Europe in an emergency. The overall mission of these forces was to contribute to a prolonged conventional defense of Western Europe on a position east of the Rhine, in the hope of repelling a major conventional offensive by the Warsaw Pact without resorting to strategic nuclear warfare. If conventional forces proved inadequate, there would be some 7,000 tactical nuclear weapons in United States custody which could be released by the President for battlefield use; but the realism of this intermediate option between conventional and strategic nuclear warfare has always been highly uncertain.

It is my opinion that the realism of a prolonged conventional defense of the present NATO front with the forces presently available is also highly uncertain. When President de Gaulle in 1966 obliged us to remove the costly line of communications that we had constructed linking the Atlantic coast of France with American forces deployed in southern Germany, we were forced to crowd most of our supply installations into the Saarbrücken area east of the French frontier. Thereafter, we have had to depend on a line of communication north to Bremerhaven which follows a route only a few miles behind the main defensive position of the allied forces. Thus, a shallow Soviet penetration of the front could quickly cut the logistic lifeline of the American Seventh Army—a penetration that could take place north of the American sector without involving a direct attack on our troops.

For years there has been a marked difference of view between the American attitude and that of our allies toward the military problems of NATO. None of the European countries except Germany has seemed particularly concerned over the many deficiencies of the allied forces resulting from differing standards of readiness, training, length of service, and logistic support among the national contingents. Thus, the ability to sustain combat has varied from sector to sector. While American leaders have long been concerned over these conditions and have urged their correction, our European colleagues have been far more relaxed. Many have been openly skeptical of the likelihood of a major conventional war and have regarded the NATO forces important more for political than for military purposes. The value of the American garrison has been as a guarantee that by its presence the United States would become involved in the early phase of any attack. The larger the American force, the more solid the guarantee of involvement appears to Europeans and the greater the credibility of our resort to nuclear weapons to protect the alliance.

If, prior to 1973, there were grounds to question the readiness of NATO forces to sustain prolonged combat, the advent of the oil crisis in that year gave added cause for pessimism. A prolonged defense of the NATO front would require continuous access to large supplies of petroleum products which only OPEC could provide. While the

Mideast oil producers might open their spigots initially, they might also turn them off at any time without notice. Even if the producers continued to supply oil, the naval protection of tanker routes from the Middle East to European ports, exposed to hostile submarines, would be both costly and precarious.

Such considerations have led me to conclude that, given the present troop dispositions, the inadequate logistic system, and the oil vulnerability of the European area, it is not reasonable to count on a prolonged conventional defense of NATO against a major attack by the Warsaw Pact forces. Furthermore, our American forces deployed in NATO, while inadequate to make a prolonged defense, are unnecessarily large to perform a mere trip-wire role which would assure American military involvement if NATO were attacked.

Let me hasten to say that this line of thinking does not lead necessarily to the conclusion that we should immediately remove or drastically reduce our military forces in Europe. To do so would further demoralize the alliance, might encourage the USSR to new probes of strength, and would dilute our political influence in Europe. As American officials have often said over the last decade or more, now is not the time to tinker with our NATO commitment. Nevertheless, in examining the changing nature of our national security, we should determine the rational dimensions of this commitment for the future and prepare to adjust it accordingly at the proper time.

In contrast to the ready combat role of our NATO forces, since our withdrawal from Vietnam the purpose of our Asian deployments has become one primarily of stabilizing Northeast Asia, indicating our continuing concern for the security of Japan, and encouraging other allies in the Western Pacific. The rather large military presence in Korea, about 40,000 men, is not justified as much by the local need for protection as by the scarcity of suitable real estate in the Far East to accommodate our troops—a shortage that seems likely to become more acute. Our new China policy has resulted in a voluntary reduction of American military personnel on Taiwan while Japanese pressures have obliged us to curtail our use of Okinawa. Since the collapse of United States policy in Southeast Asia, political forces are developing which threaten our military eviction from Thailand and the Philippines. So if we aspire to exercise any significant military influence in this part of the world in the future, we must try to retain our general purpose forces in size and location essentially as at present.

In appraising the need for overseas deployments in the future, economic considerations will have to be taken increasingly into account. In a competitive world vying for scarce materials, a military presence in proximity to important overseas sources of imports may assume considerable importance. While we are fortunate to have most of our foreign sources in the Western Hemisphere, there are some in faraway places like Australia, Malaysia, and southern Africa. In the case of oil, if we expect to achieve early independence from Mideast sources, we must cultivate good relations with producers elsewhere such as in Nigeria and Indonesia as well as in the Western Hemisphere.

In addition to deciding upon the dimensions of the NATO commitment and of our Asian deployments, security policy makers must also determine the capabilities desired of the central reserve at home. In particular, what should be the size, composition, and purpose of a quick reaction force (QRF) which can go into combat overseas as fast as strategic transport can be made available to move it?

One must recognize at the outset that it is unsafe to count on early reinforcements from the Reserves either because their units are unlikely to be combat-ready in time or because the President may not obtain congressional consent to mobilize them. There will be no draft to provide reinforcements until Congress passes a new conscription law and until the inductees thereunder have completed six months of training. Hence, if our leaders are prudent, they will plan to send into action promptly only those Regular forces of the central reserve that can look after themselves for three to six months with little help beyond the regular establishment. If the task overseas exceeds the capability of this limited force, the President will have to stay his military hand for the time necessary to mobilize and ready a larger one.

If there is to be an orderly mobilization plan, it will be essential to get an authoritative decision on this important point—whether, as I recommend, to plan on the prompt dispatch of a small Regular force to deal with a sudden emergency overseas or to accept considerable delay while preparing a mixed Regular-Reserve force of larger size. At present we are planning on a mixed force heavily dependent on Reserves but without acknowledging the inevitability of considerable delay in assuring the combat readiness of such a force.

In distributing budgetary resources among the services, Pentagon authorities must bear in mind the numerous demanding tasks which will fall to the Navy in this period. It will be expected to neutralize the submarine threat to our shores and vital sea communications, to protect the overseas movement and supply of military forces, and to assure continued commercial access to essential overseas markets. If, as seems likely, the limits of national territorial waters will be extended to 200 miles and American companies become active in exploring and exploiting the riches of the sea bed, the Navy will acquire a new set of responsibilities in protecting the sea areas involved.

This expansion of Navy missions has already created a demand for a bigger fleet which, in turn, has stimulated a sharp debate over the kind of ships that will be required. Will the emphasis be on large nuclear-powered surface ships and supersubmarines of the *Trident* type, each costing a billion dollars or more? Or will it be on numbers of smaller, cheaper, faster craft to permit a widened naval presence in the expanding sea areas of our new interests? If the budget limits postulated in this book are to be respected, it seems certain that some middle course must be adopted which will assure a considerable increase in number of ships.

To carry out the economy-related tasks of the Navy, there must be close liaison between economic and military planners. The economists will need to determine the location of areas of future economic interest, taking into account the military difficulties of assuring access to them. Accessibility in this sense is a function of distance from the United States, port facilities available in the area, and exposure of sea lanes to foreign interdiction by political, economic, military or terrorist means. Such considerations underline the importance of developing supply sources outside of politically unfriendly neighborhoods and, in the case of oil, of finding reliable sources outside of the Mideast. Also, it must be remembered that sea communications cannot be secured at all times in all places. The Navy must be given clear priorities among its many tasks—there will never be enough ships to do everything concurrently.

Once authoritative decisions have been obtained on the future size and purpose of our NATO-committed forces, on the quick reaction mission of the central reserve, and on the priority of naval tasks in policing the seas, our security planners will be ready to proceed with a broad design of the conventional forces. In the absence of official guidance, I would propose to use criteria of sufficiency based on the considerations raised in our previous discussions. Under these terms, adequate conventional forces would have the ability (a) to fulfill a reduced NATO commitment and maintain Asian ground-air deployments at about 100,000 men located primarily in Korea, Okinawa, and the Philippines; (b) to maintain a central reserve capable of promptly dispatching overseas a multidivisional QRF able to sustain itself for three to six months with little help from Reserves; (c) to provide Navy-Marine forces necessary to support the foregoing activities and to protect designated sea communications of primary military and economic importance; and (d) to provide permanent garrisons of appropriate size for Panama and Alaska. These forces must be supportable within an overall military budget representing about 8 per cent of the GNP and within a personnel strength amounting to approximately 2.1 million men. If, after efforts to meet these standards, the security planners find that the funds or the manpower are insufficient to produce such forces, they should be required to suggest a reduction of tasks to make missions compatible with force capability.

Having played the role of supreme authority in establishing the criteria to be met by the conventional forces, I cannot complain if now obliged to make specific recommendations as to the mission and composition of their principal components. I am willing to make the effort in the case of the overseas deployments and the central reserve of Army–Air Forces in the United States. In the case of naval forces, I am obliged to plead lack of qualification to express other than very general views. (As I have often told my admiral friends, most Americans are quite sure of their ability to be a general but are inclined to diffidence when it comes to being an admiral.)

To comply with the first criterion for the conventional forces, we must propose a modified form of our present NATO commitment, one that will recognize the infeasibility of a prolonged defense of the present position east of the Rhine and the untenable position of the American forces resulting from their exposed line of communication. Any new solution must take into account certain facts which are unlikely to change. To begin with, our allies will never contribute the manpower and money necessary to make the present front truly defensible. Neither NATO, France, nor the American Congress will pay the bill to restore the American line of communications across France that was lost in 1966. Germany will never willingly consent to a withdrawal of the main line of defense behind the Rhine. The availability of tactical nuclear weapons is likely to remain clouded by uncertainty regarding Presidential release of these weapons for use, and doubt about the agreement of European nations to use them against targets on their soil. Finally, while Congress will probably withhold action for a while in the wake of our Asian defeat, it is sure to impose a cut in European deployments in the reasonably near future if the Executive branch does not take the initiative.

If these assumptions are indeed facts, as I believe them to be, the alternatives open to consideration are quite restricted. One, of course, is to change the present NATO strategy to a trip-wire defense on the ground backed only by the threat of strategic nuclear weapons. This concept was properly rejected years ago at a time when the United States had an unquestioned strategic superiority over the USSR. There is much less to recommend it at a time of U.S.-Soviet strategic parity.

Given the foregoing assumptions, my preferred solution would be to reduce our present forces by about a half, reposition them on a line of communications with a chance of survival, and adjust our defensive expectations accordingly. We would reorganize our Army forces into a corps of two divisions and locate them in the Frankfurt area with a line of communications to Antwerp. The corps would retain the present three armored cavalry regiments to screen the sector frontier, eject minor incursions, and delay the advance of larger forces. All military dependents would be sent home and the units would rotate by battalion after a service of about six months.

Concurrently, there would be a program to modernize but reduce the number of tactical nuclear weapons while simplifying the procedure by which the President releases these weapons for use. To provide a reinforcement in conventional fire power, we could introduce large numbers of the new high-precision ("smart") bombs and rockets which have proved so effective in Vietnam and the Mideast.

If this proposal could gain acceptance at home and in the alliance it would have many advantages, some already mentioned. It would place our reduced forces in a more tenable location, linked to the Channel by a shorter and less exposed line of communications. With about half of our present forces and all dependents withdrawn to the United States, our stake in an illusory conventional defense east of the Rhine would be prudently limited and the strength regained would be placed in reserve in the United States where it could be of effective use in an emergency—possibly in NATO. At the same time, it would assure NATO forces of the best available weapons, conventional and nuclear, for inflicting losses on an enemy before it arrived at close grips with the ground forces. Finally, we would protect NATO from the disruptive effects of an abrupt, impetuous decision of Congress to bring most of our forces home.

If this proposal were put into effect, the costs associated with it should be moderate. The reduction in military personnel would decrease costs as would the removal of dependents. On the other hand, new expenditures would be required to reposition the troops and their supplies in the Frankfurt area and to complete a line of communications to Antwerp. Unit rotation would probably prove somewhat more costly than the present system. Only the Comptroller of the Department of Defense could make a reliable estimate of the net cost of the readjustment but in the end on a world-wide basis we would achieve significantly more security from our military resources.

I have no illusion that such a proposal could escape strong opposition in NATO unless the time were right and the reasons for it persuasively presented. It might be related to a concurrent reduction of Soviet forces or to a revised defensive strategy replacing the present linear defense with a hedgehog disposition of strong points protected by nuclear and conventional fire. It might be urged as the best way to avoid a disruptive congressional initiative.

We might find other things to make the proposal more attractive to our colleagues. We could guarantee to keep a force ready to send back to Europe to restore the strength of the American contingent to at least its present level. We could offer naval assistance in keeping open the tanker routes between the Mideast oil fields and NATO consumers. If additional evidence of American concern for Europe were necessary, we might propose a widening of the military alliance to include closer political and economic collaboration. After all, if we take the position that national security is no longer exclusively a military matter the same should be true for the security of NATO.

As for our Asian deployments, we could hardly expect to convince Japan and other allies in the Western Pacific of the seriousness of our interest in their region with forces smaller than those now there—roughly the Seventh Fleet, one army and one marine division, and associated air units distributed among Korea, Japan, Okinawa, and the Philippines. As a matter of fact, it would not be easy to find suitable areas of deployment of larger forces if we so desired. However, the role of the permanent overseas garrisons could be supplemented by military exercises carried out sometimes jointly with the armed forces of local allies.

The most difficult element of the conventional forces to structure is the central reserve in the United States, primarily because of the numerous roles that it may be called on to fulfill. It should contain a QRF capable of reinforcing NATO or other overseas garrisons, of defending the primary security zone in the Western Hemisphere and its approaches, and of providing a relatively small expeditionary force for intervention at a greater distance where our interests may come in conflict with those of the USSR or of lesser adversaries.

On the other hand, the central reserve might become the advance guard of larger forces which the nation mobilized to meet contingencies beyond the unaided capabilities of volunteer forces. The United States has always maintained large Reserve components at great expense to permit waging major conventional war on the model of World War II or Korea. Of all the military services, the Army is the most dependent on Reserves, maintaining some 400,000 in the National Guard and about half that number in the Army Reserve, at a cost of over $2 billion a year. During most of my service, mobilization plans were based on having Regular Army forces capable of moving overseas at once on the outbreak of war and Reserve units ready to follow on their heels in an endless stream until the military need was met in full. The factor controlling the rate of deployment was assumed to be the availability of strategic transport, naval and air.

Insofar as the Army was concerned, there were several things wrong with this concept. The first was the impossibility in practice of maintaining Reserve combat units at the necessary level of readiness, a point I have made previously. The second was the assumption that the Regular forces would be kept "balanced"—that is, a proper ratio would be maintained between the combat forces (largely infantry, artillery, and armor) and the supporting services (engineers, communications, transportation, medical, etc.). In time of peace when defense budgets are meager, there is every temptation to maintain more combat units, called "teeth" in modern Pentagon vernacular, in contrast to "tail," the noncombat elements which are nonetheless indispensable to the effective performance of the combat forces. This practice has been regarded as good domestic politics—"we eliminate the fat and keep the muscle"—and also the increased number of divisions is thought to add to the military posture which impresses an enemy. Just as numbers of strategic weapons seem to radiate a certain mystique, so do numbers of divisions. However, in a crisis a

shortage of supporting forces in the Regular establishment may delay
sending an expedition overseas or oblige undue dependence on reinforcing units composed of insufficiently trained Reserves.

A third fallacy in the endless-stream mobilization concept has been
a chronic underestimation of the time required to establish a logistic
base overseas necessary to support continuous military operations by
American forces with their sophisticated equipment and high rates
of consumption. Early in the Vietnam war, hawkish critics of U.S.
policy complained of the slow rate of deployment of American forces
to South Vietnam once it had been decided to commit them. Actually that rate was usually about as fast as permitted by the state of
the logistic preparations to receive and support them. A modern army
still marches on a stomach with an insatiable appetite for food,
ammunition, and gasoline which requires an efficiently functioning
logistic base for satisfaction. The outcome of modern wars is increasingly a matter of logistics, a factor that dominates strategy and tactics
by setting bounds of feasibility to the scope, duration, intensity, and
location of military operations.

The foregoing comments are necessary to explain my concept of
a proper mobilization plan for the future and its effect on the organization of the central reserve. From the resources available to the
latter, I would try to form a balanced QRF of about five divisions,
with the appropriate air component, ready to fight in NATO or in
any other area of strategic importance where the United States might
be obliged to send military forces. Organic equipment provided these
forces would be that always required wherever fighting might occur.
Expensive equipment needed only intermittently or only in certain
geographical areas or climates (for example, tanks, certain types of
aircraft, helicopters, heavy trucks, amphibious equipment for landing
on hostile shores, and special engineer equipment) would be kept in
equipment pools to be drawn out only when the need was anticipated. Experience in Korea and Vietnam has demonstrated that
equipment designed primarily to fight Russians in Western Europe
is often of limited use in underdeveloped countries against indigenous
enemies.

The residual force of the central reserve beyond the QRF would include not only units, individuals, and supplies necessary to replace losses in the QRF but also four additional understrength divisions which could be brought to a high state of readiness within three months after a mobilization of the Reserves. These four divisions would eventually become a second QRF ready for the next contingency that might arise, possibly the reinforcement of the original QRF. In the meantime it would serve as a Hemisphere reserve watching over the primary security zone.

Within this residual force there would be a counterterror organization to which all services would make contributions. It would consist of specially trained commando groups capable of operating on the ground, at sea, or in the air. Their specialty would be to cope with the many forms of international terrorist and criminal activities which have been or may be used for political purposes—assassination, the taking and killing of hostages, skyjacking, the seizure of nuclear explosives, illegal trafficking in drugs, industrial sabotage, and acts of piracy. Here is a new and highly important field for the armed forces which will require an unusual degree of versatility and innovative skill on the part of the participants.

By this line of reasoning, the central reserve would have need for about nine army divisions, the first five of which, with balancing noncombat units and air support, would be immediately ready. Counting the two divisions in NATO and one in Korea, we have thus established a need for roughly twelve Army divisions, plus a few brigades equal to at least one division for the permanent protection of Panama and Alaska. As oil production increases in Alaska, it may become necessary to strengthen that garrison to provide protection for both oil fields and pipelines.

I have focused attention on Army forces since the Army division is a convenient and customary unit (though often misleading) for measuring a nation's ability to wage conventional war. Needless to say, these Army divisions will require the support of units of the Tactical Air Force of a strength proportionate to the Army forces involved and the resistance expected from the enemy. Also, there are two Marine divisions, one located on each coast, which I have not accounted for. In the past, they have been regarded as reserved for duty afloat with the Navy or for situations involving amphibious operations. In practice, they have been used in specific situations in accordance with common sense, sometimes in a purely Army role.*

I can evaluate only very roughly the size and kind of Air Force necessary to give the proper balance to these conventional forces. The ratio of tactical aircraft to army divisions would probably remain about the same, but the tactics and weapons required for the ground support mission must take into account the growing lethality of antiaircraft weapons available to ground forces. I would expect American army forces soon to be able to take over their own protection against enemy aircraft flying at low and medium altitudes provided that all such planes could be assumed hostile and hence fair game for army weapons. In providing strategic air transport for Army forces, the Air Force will have an expanding mission as the central reserve grows in size and the submarine threat to surface shipping increases the dangers in certain sea areas.

Elsewhere I have paid tribute to the added importance of the Navy in a period of increasing economic dependence on foreign trade. This increase of possible tasks necessitates a finer definition of missions, particularly with respect to the control of the sea lanes. Past language in official Defense literature may be interpreted as directing the Navy to protect not only our vital sea areas but also those of our European

---

*Summary of divisions and eventual location in the recommended force structure:
Army Divisions—12, plus 1 Division Equivalent

Overseas:
NATO, 2
Korea, 1
In U.S. (including Panama):
Quick Reaction Force, 5
Residual divisions, in central reserve, 4
Garrisons of Alaska and Panama, 3 brigades equivalent to 1 division
Marine Divisions—3
Overseas:
Okinawa, 1
In U.S.: 2
Total Army/Marine Corps Divisions—16

and Pacific allies. In time of war, despite the proliferation of Soviet submarines, the Navy would remain charged with keeping the sea lanes open to Europe against a maximum Soviet interdiction effort. There has been no abatement in the Navy-Marine requirement to be ready to wage amphibious warfare after the manner of World War II despite the low probability of the mission. Meanwhile, Congress and some Executive officials are supporting the concept of a virtually all-nuclear fleet despite the cost implications.

At a time when we shall undoubtedly need a Navy of more than 500 ships, its present approximate size, the open-ended official guidance contained in statements of Navy missions invites excessive budget requests which, if granted, would disrupt the balance of ground, sea, and air power needed to perform the major military functions required for our security. While the Pentagon should never resort to allocating frozen percentages of the military budget to the services, important changes in annual allocations should be weighed thoughtfully and effected only for good reason. The role of the armed forces in waging and deterring war is a composite task requiring effective contributions from all services. In the words of President Eisenhower in 1958, "The waging of war by separate ground, sea, and air forces is gone forever."

To summarize, the conventional forces proposed for the military component of the national security program would have essentially the same personnel strength as at present, but eventually a smaller deployment in Europe and a substantially larger central reserve in the United States. The latter would maintain a quick reaction all-Regular force of about five divisions for immediate movement overseas by a combination of air and sea transport. This force could be followed by four additional Regular divisions with a large Reserve component after from three to six months. Thereafter, we would have to depend on the Reserves and initially untrained manpower to support a prolonged major war.

The Army required in such a program would amount to about thirteen divisions, made stronger by modern equipment and adequate reserves of supplies necessary to sustain war and to assist allies. A tactical Air Force would be maintained, one modified to meet the new conditions to be anticipated on the modern battlefield, along with a larger strategic airlift to give mobility to the central reserve. The Navy would increase in numbers of vessels while struggling to strike a balance between a desire for large and costly nuclear-propelled ships and the obvious need of many more ships to patrol the vast ocean spaces which will contain our vital economic interests. All services would recognize the growing danger of international terrorism and violence and prepare specialized forces to cope with them.

VIII

The Civil Component
of National Security

In a previous chapter we considered some of the shortcomings of national power and identified weaknesses in the nonmilitary component. One point made was that a President has only contingent access to most of the resources of this sector and that those derived from the national economy in particular are often beyond his reach. Since the economy is largely privately owned, its assets are quite properly out of range of government intervention except as specifically authorized by law. While no true believer in the free enterprise system would want to remove this restriction, it puts our government at a distinct disadvantage in dealing with adversaries who can wage economic or monetary warfare against us with little danger of prompt retaliation in kind.

We have also called attention to the wasting of power in the operation of the Executive machinery, much of it arising from organizational defects, ill-trained or inexperienced officials in key positions, and the absence of any mechanism like the National Security Council to integrate the efforts of several elements of government contributing to a common course of action. In designing the civil component of a national security policy, we must try to find ways to correct or at least attenuate these defects.

The nonmilitary resources available for the purposes of national security are found primarily in the Chief Executive (as contrasted to the Commander in Chief), the Department of State including the Agency for International Development, the United States Information Agency, and the loosely confederated Executive departments and independent agencies dealing with economic, fiscal-monetary, and welfare programs. The intelligence community also contributes insofar as it produces information from overseas bearing on the activities of these civil agencies. As in the case of the military component, we may properly ask what support we would like from these elements to enhance national security.

Since we are accustomed to demanding the impossible of a President, we might simply ask him as Chief Executive to exercise his power wisely and effectively in accordance with law and the Constitution in formulating national policy. The yardstick to apply to his choices of policy goals and programs would be that which should be used to verify the authenticity of any presumptive national interest —will the probable national gain from success exceed by a safe margin the costs and risks to be anticipated? To answer this question he will need a well-trained staff to suggest various alternatives, analyze their advantages and disadvantages, and help him arrive at an enlightened choice based on the facts available. The rightness of his eventual choice will probably have to await the judgment of impartial historians years after the event—in their retrospective eye, today's apparent victories or defeats may assume a different aspect.

If a President is to perform his traditional function of spokesman of the government before the people and chief advocate of United States policy before the outside world, he must become more adept in the arts of communication and opinion formation than most of his recent forbears. If, as a current slogan asserts, "the people have a right to know," they have a right to look to their President as the primary source of information regarding the actions and intentions of the government. As noted elsewhere, it is not easy for him to play this part. Unless he speaks out effectively, the molding of public opinion will be left largely to the media, often committed to an adversary attitude toward his policies and accustomed to exercising partisan selectivity in deciding what news deserves public attention. To counter these powerful and often rival sources of information, a President has immediately available only his personal gifts of advocacy, occasionally reinforced by the voices of political colleagues and echoed by the Press Secretary at the White House. Whereas a British Prime Minister wishing to rally his constituents can use the floor of Parliament as a sounding board, a President appears before Congress only infrequently to report on the state of the union or some similarly broad subject. If he wants to talk to the nation on a current issue of lesser magnitude he must somehow obtain TV time from the big networks and expect to receive instant rebuttal from critics waiting in the wings to attack his case.

In the American political system, it is not easy to find ways for a President to hold his own against media adversaries with their control of the principal means of opinion formation. During the Johnson administration, I suggested an arrangement whereby the TV and radio networks would be asked to set aside an hour or two of prime time each week to allow a recurrent public questioning of the President or his senior officials on important matters of current interest. Such a device could work to the advantage of the public, the media, and the administration, affording the latter both the advantages and the tribulations of Parliamentary interpellation so useful in the British political system. The questioners could be congressmen, media representatives, or "concerned citizens" with the issues for discussion picked in advance by the White House or by some form of public or congressional poll. This procedure could have considerable appeal as a means for allowing the public to cross-examine their senior servants under conditions permitting thoughtful answers to serious questions.

A final requirement to place upon the President would be for him to install an Executive mechanism for integrating nonmilitary power into national programs—something analogous to the National Security Council in the foreign-military sector. Such an innovation would require strong Presidential support to overcome the resistance of entrenched bureaucrats and congressional committees with a vested interest in the Executive status quo. Such forces accounted in large measure for the failure of the State Department in 1966–1968 to exploit the primacy in overseas activities accorded the Secretary by President Johnson in the text of National Security Action Memorandum 341. In it, the President designated the Secretary of State as his agent to direct, coordinate, and supervise all interdepartmental activities overseas. Unfortunately, senior State officials were so lethargic in implementing this grant of authority that the results of the new procedure were unimpressive, so much so that the Nixon administration lost little time in sweeping most of it away and returning to the White House the responsibilities that President Johnson had conceded to State. This was the beginning of the decline of State's institutional influence on foreign policy, which continues at present writing.

These comments lead to a consideration of what we should want from diplomacy in support of national security. We would, of course, want the diplomats to produce sound advice and innovative recommendations to assist the President in his major foreign policy decisions. We would hope that in addition to the traditional skills of their profession—the use of persuasion, inducement, threats, cajolery, and guile as required for advancing national interests, there would be in their ranks men of executive ability capable as ambassadors of directing large and complex overseas missions including representation of several federal departments and able to supervise programs often unrelated to diplomacy.

In the anticipated environment, our senior State officials must pay greater attention to economic issues than in the past. As I have observed the activities of the Executive branch, State's participation in economic policy has been indirect or peripheral. During my Pentagon service, it was Defense officials who took the lead in negotiating agreements with NATO countries for the reimbursement of U.S. expenditures for the maintenance of troops in Europe or in arranging sales of equipment to allies to reduce the chronic deficit in our balance of payments. My impression was that Treasury officials normally dealt with foreign governments on monetary matters with little participation of State other than in arranging the proper contacts with foreign officials. Although in the foreign intelligence field, State originally had responsibility for collecting economic intelligence, it eventually withdrew from this activity in favor of the Central Intelligence Agency. Hereafter, we would want senior State officials to recognize the value of economic and monetary tools in advancing national policy and the need to develop a facility in using them as effective weapons with which to induce or coerce a stubborn opponent. A timely grant of access to the United States grain or computer market may be more effective in influencing a foreign government than some brilliant *démarche* or stern ultimatum.

While the opportunity presents itself, we might place two additional requests on State in the name of national security. We should require it to undertake a continuing review of all our alliances and commitments to assure that they are still relevant to our current needs and interests. I would say that at this moment many would not meet this criterion. Most of them were consummated at a time when our primary concern was the containment of world communism, a concern which, while not outmoded, has been somewhat tempered by schismatic developments within the postwar Communist bloc and the so-called *détente* in East-West relations.

In the meantime, we have acquired new problems requiring cooperative assistance from allies—problems arising from the OPEC oil cartel, inflation and recession in the industrialized world, and the consequences of the population explosioin in the underdeveloped countries. Most of these problems have national and international aspects requiring concurrent solutions in many countries to be effective.

To cope with such matters we shall need cooperation and support from many nations that in the past have not been formally allied to us. Our relations with our neighbors, Mexico and Canada, will always be important, particularly with the latter, which is by far the most important source of our imported raw materials. For assured access to Mideast oil, we shall need to be on good terms with Saudi Arabia, and Iran. In Africa, we will be interested in Nigerian petroleum and the minerals in South and West Africa. In South America, Brazil and Venezuela will loom large in our political and economic eye—Brazil for its size and natural resources, Venezuela for its oil and accumulating wealth. For similar reasons we should watch the development of Indonesia and make it occasional tenders of friendship. Bearing in mind that the Western Hemisphere contains most of our primary security zone, State should endeavor to eradicate the feeling in most of Latin America that it is an ignored part of the world which we tend to take for granted.

A final requirement to lay upon the diplomatic sector is the development of an improved breed of professional negotiators able to defend our interests at the bargaining table with the same dedication that good soldiers display on the battlefield. Our record in this field since World War II has not been impressive—particularly not in the endurance tests with Communist polemicists in Panmunjom and Paris over terms to end the armed conflicts in Korea and Vietnam. We needed then, and shall need in the future, diplomats imbued with the lessons derived from case studies of past contests and trained to wage negotiations with the same patient determination as their toughest adversaries, giving nothing away without getting something in return and resisting the temptation to yield on key issues in order to carry home some kind of agreement.

From the economic-fiscal-monetary sector of the Executive we should demand continuing study and research of the long-term economic problems of a great industrialized nation in a congesting world plagued by too many people consuming too much too fast for the lagging production of food, energy, and manufactured goods. From such studies, we would hope for timely, comprehensive programs to forestall future shortages, to provide substitutes for scarce items, and to press technology to its limits to moderate the consequences of excess population. Specifically, we shall want an adequate energy program to attain eventual independence from foreign oil, one which has been promised now for years and still is undelivered. Also, we shall look to the economic sector to devise a system of adequate record keeping on all important economic activities, hoping thereby to furnish responsible officials with a solid basis of facts and operational data to assist them in reaching wise solutions.

Since we have become accustomed to thinking of national security programs as rivals for resources of those in support of national well-being, it may seem surprising to expect a contribution to national security from the welfare sector of the Executive. The fact is that national well-being often plays a supporting role to national security and the reverse is also true. To assure our economic and social well-being, we must provide security for the valuables which contribute thereto, and, for that security, we must be willing to pay a very considerable price in resources. But to justify such a sacrifice for security, our people must appreciate the extent of their well-being and be determined to retain it—by military force if necessary. Thus security and well-being are mutually supporting; in fact, they are the opposite faces of a single coin of great value to the individual and the nation and both represent causes worthy of loyal support.

If we are to employ to the fullest the nonmilitary resources dispersed throughout the Executive branch, means must be found to draw them together in a way to permit centralized planning, programming, and supervision of progress. The absence of any organization for this purpose recalls the condition of the autonomous, loosely related military services prior to 1947. Until the National Security Act of that year the Army, Navy, and the inchoate Air Force went pretty much their separate ways, each preparing for a kind of war consistent with individual capabilities and inclinations with no directive authority short of the President. This condition ended only after the establishment of a strong Department of Defense and adoption of a task force concept for organizing the combat elements of the three services for military operations.

The present problem of strengthening the exposed civil flank of national security is somewhat analogous. We can no longer pursue relatively independent foreign, military, economic, fiscal-monetary, and welfare policies conducted with limited coordination yet supported by contributions from a single central pool of resources. Instead, we need an integrated national policy of many ingredients blended in proper combination to support specific policy goals and to overcome anticipated obstacles. If we are to reach solutions for the many difficult problems awaiting us, we shall need to provide in advance an orderly procedure for effecting this integration of effort.

A number of ways of doing so would be possible if we were willing to undertake a complete overhaul of the federal government, starting with a new constituent assembly to write a constitution embodying all the lessons learned in the first two centuries of the Republic. But we could hardly expect the expeditious action displayed by the Convention of 1787; the mere time factor in getting a consensus today on the many controversial issues that would arise is enough to discourage such a procedure.

Thus, we are obliged to consider remedial courses of action within the present Constitution, preferably without having to seek amendments or much new legislation. Adherence to this approach would focus attention on ways to recombine what we have within the present governmental structure without disturbing existing departmental responsibilities and boundaries. The effort to centralize authority and responsibility would be limited to policy research and to the planning, programming, and coordination of multidepartmental actions. The responsibility for implementing actions would remain that of the departments presently responsible.

Seeking to adapt existing relationships where possible rather than to create new ones, one might consider assigning the integrating function to the cabinet which, in the words of the *United States Government Organization Manual*, "is a creation of custom and tradition, going back to the First President, and functions at the pleasure of the President." However, in recent administrations, no President has ever assigned the cabinet a significant role in the field of overall domestic policy or provided it with a supporting staff beyond a cabinet Secretary to permit it to assume a more important role. Whatever the reason, it has not been the pleasure of recent

Presidents to use it for matters of broad policy—a fact which justifies looking elsewhere for the integrating mechanism we are seeking.

Next, we turn to consideration of the National Security Council, which has the advantage of being a statutory body that has served since 1947 as a mechanism to coordinate policy in the foreign-military field. In the language of the National Security Act of 1947, the NSC is charged with "advising the President with respect to the integration of domestic, foreign and military policies related to national security." If we give to national security the broadened meaning advocated in this book, this language, by its reference to domestic policy, would justify assigning to the present National Security Council the task of coordinating all interdepartmental efforts, military and nonmilitary, in the name of national security.

But at least two objections would arise to such a proposal. In the past, as I have mentioned, the National Security Council has limited itself to matters of foreign and military policy with little attention being paid to the civil or domestic sector, about which we are presently concerned. If, with its present name and charter unchanged, the National Security Council suddenly expanded its scope to include most of the policies and issues of the civil sector, there would be a dismayed cry that the partisans of foreign policy and of military solutions had taken over the Executive branch to the prejudice of liberal issues providing for domestic welfare and social justice. One could also object that the present statutory membership of the National Security Council provides no representation for the senior spokesmen for these threatened causes.

My solution would be to terminate the National Security Council in its present form and name, replacing it by a National Policy Council (NPC), which would retain the useful parts of the old structure but broaden its membership and role. The change in name would emphasize that all national policy, including all aspects of national security and well-being, are henceforth the subject matter of the new agency. This fact would be further recognized by inclusion of the Secretaries of the Treasury and Health, Education, and Welfare in the membership along with the four present members of the

National Security Council—the President, Vice-President, and Secretaries of State and Defense. To represent the economy, the President would nominate for Senate approval a seventh member, whom I shall call the Economic Representative of the President (Ec-Rep). He might come from the ranks of senior officialdom or from private life, but regardless of provenance he would soon become an important figure on the Washington scene; hence, the Senate should approve his appointment.

With this membership, the NPC would contain representation of the four principal sectors of national policy: (1) foreign-military-intelligence; (2) economic; (3) fiscal-monetary; and (4) domestic welfare. For each sector it would need a subordinate panel chaired respectively by the Secretary of State, the Ec-Rep, the Secretary of the Treasury, and the Secretary of Health, Education, and Welfare. Panel members would be the heads (or deputies) of the departments and agencies with major responsibilities in the sector represented by the panel. Panel chairmen would be free to invite other officials to attend on specific occasions because of their interest in an item on the agenda.

I would imagine that these panels would become the scene of highly important activities involving frequent surveys of present and future problems in the zone of panel responsibility. Panel 1 would be immersed in such perennials as foreign commitments and alliances, the coordination of military and foreign policy, international population growth, arms limitation, the control of proliferation of nuclear weapons, and the quality of national intelligence. Panel 2 would deal with many of the economic problems that plague us: inflation, recession, unemployment, and sources of energy. To these issues would be progressively added others arising from growing shortages in food, natural resources, and raw materials. Panel 3 would seek ways to balance governmental expenditures and income without mortgaging our national future, to stimulate adequate capital formation, and to maintain a sound currency and adequate money supply. Panel 4 should make provision for meeting the growing needs for health, educational, and social services and to ameliorate the effects of excessive urbanization.

At time of writing, a national debate centers about the role of the CIA and ways and means to exercise Executive and congressional control over this supersecret agency. Under the National Policy Council concept, I would propose relieving the present Director of Central Intelligence (renamed Director of Foreign Intelligence) of all direct responsibility for the CIA, and making him a member of panel 1 and Chief Intelligence Officer of the government. He would take with him from the CIA the U.S. Intelligence Board and all the functions of the present Director of Central Intelligence involving the coordination, evaluation, and dissemination of national intelligence relating to national security. He would operate from offices somewhere near the White House and would be responsible to the National Policy Council via panel 1 for the effective operation of the intelligence community in the production of national intelligence.

Panel 1 would replace the present National Security Council Intelligence Committee and assume responsibility for evaluating the quality of national intelligence and for verifying compliance with law, policy, and regulations on the part of CIA and the remainder of the intelligence community. It would function somewhat as the present "40" Committee in approving or rejecting covert operations proposed by the CIA but would supervise and appraise their execution more closely than in the past.

The new Director, CIA, would have the sole responsibility of directing, managing, and supervising the CIA in the execution of its assigned responsibilities. He would be a member of the U.S. Intelligence Board and deputy chairman to the Director of Foreign Intelligence. For intelligence matters he would report directly to the Director of Foreign Intelligence; for covert operations, to panel 1. Such an arrangement would give him more time to concentrate on the internal workings of the Agency and an opportunity to exercise firmer control over the lower echelons of his organization.

One final comment on the intelligence system. It would be important for the National Policy Council to specify formally that the Director of Foreign Intelligence should function purely as an intelligence specialist, never as a foreign policy adviser to the President. The official responsible for intelligence should have no personal commitment to the outcome of policy debate—any such involvement could have unintended effects in biasing his reporting and interpretation of intelligence.

Under this proposal, would there be adequate surveillance of the covert operations, i.e., the "dirty tricks" of the CIA? I would assume that the NPC would give the CIA clearer and more restrictive guidelines than those under which the Agency has operated in the past, also that the authority of the inspector general within the CIA will be greatly strengthened. Then, with closer supervision of specific projects by panel, 1, I would feel that reorganization has done about all it can to improve control of the Agency. In the long run, for assurance that a clandestine service like the CIA will always operate properly in the manner intended by law, the President must depend largely on the personal integrity of the key officials of the agency. While organizational changes may help, the solution of the CIA problem will rest in the quality of its people.

How will it be possible to develop the knowledge and expertise within the NPC required to cope with the a wide range of complex problems that it will confront? First there must be a Council staff, headed by an able Staff Director to supervise its internal functioning, prepare the agenda for Council meetings, verify the readiness of papers for presentation to it, record the President's decisions, disseminate orders to the proper agencies for implementation, and follow up on progress in executing them.

Next, there must be a procedure for collecting, interpreting, and storing all forms of data and information needed to support the work of the Council and of the panels. The existing intelligence community, headed by the Director of Foreign Intelligence, can be assigned responsibility for information from foreign sources; but no mechanism exists for performing this task at home. The function could be centralized at the level of the National Policy Council, decentralized to the panels, or assigned to some newly created agency external to the Council, conceivably servicing both the Council and certain committees of Congress. After all, it would be helpful if Executive and congressional agencies working in the same domestic field had access to the same facts. At the start, I would favor decentralizing the function to the panels pending the development of some experience in operating the Council.

Another matter of great importance would be the manner of conducting research and continuous studies in the fields of long-lived problems—activities which would draw on all relevant resources of science, scholarship, and historical experience and in so doing reinforce the in-house capabilities of the Council staff. How to satisfy this need for deep research and anticipatory study is a question that invites innovative proposals. My own suggestion would be to create a Center for Policy Research, which would borrow from the experience and procedures of two widely dissimilar institutions, the National Institutes of Health and the National War College. The Center would have as its overall purpose a study of the causes, prevention, and cures of some of the principal ills of government, economy, and society, and the formulation of policies for coping with them in their present and projected forms. A collateral responsibility would be the training of officials for future participation in research programs and policy formulation. Thus, it would have two main divisions: one for policy research, the other for the instruction of advanced students in policy formulation.

The Center would report to the National Policy Council through the Staff Director and prepare studies on its own initiative or upon request from the Council or from one of the panels. The students would be officials chosen by their departments of origin to serve as interns, learning on the job the arcana of policy making. The study, research, and teaching personnel would come from government or from extramural academic or research communities. Outside consultants could be hired or contracts granted to "think tanks" to obtain additional help on special projects.

To summarize the foregoing discussion, my proposal is to replace the National Security Council by a National Policy Council to serve as a forum of broad discussion and as a mechanism for recommending policies and programs to the President while maintaining a continuing study of long-term problems across the entire spectrum of Executive responsibilities. The seven-man Council would be supported by four panels manned by selected cabinet heads and by a Center for Policy Research made up of study groups of specialists concentrating on long-term problems. The Center would also provide on-the-job instruction to officials assigned to acquire experience in policy formulation and to improve their professional value as career public servants. For the first time in history, the Executive branch would have in the National Policy Council a ready means for tapping all sources of available power and blending the varied contributions of many departments for maximum effect in supporting all aspects of national policy.

While the proposal to create a National Policy Council to replace the National Security Council is relatively simple to carry out without greatly disturbing the present configuration of the Executive branch, it would raise objections from many quarters, both from bureaucrats instinctively resistant to change in old and familiar ways and from citizens who would find cause for genuine foreboding in certain of its aspects. Within the ranks of State and Defense, there are those who would oppose a widening of the old National Security Council, which might expose military and foreign programs and budgets to sharper criticism and closer scrutiny from those elements of the Executive with a primary concern for domestic welfare. Partisans of social causes, in turn, would feel uneasy about presenting their case before a forum until recently dominated by representatives of foreign-military interests with a long experience in using the machinery of the National Security Council to their advantage.

There would be those fearful of giving greater powers to the Presidency after the abuses revealed in the Watergate scandals. Some would interpret the proposal as giving the President greater control over civil activities, the economy in particular, and thus inviting government intervention in industry and business to a degree hitherto unknown in peacetime. It might be said that the collection and storing of the data required by the National Policy Council would result in added invasions of individual and corporate privacy and encourage further Big Brother prying. Finally, economic planning on the scale proposed carries the unpleasant suggestion of a welfare or socialist state.

Congress would certainly perceive these possibilities and would demand satisfaction on all such points as a condition for concurrence in the changes proposed. It is most unlikely that Congress would be willing to adjust its own committee organizations to dovetail with the panels of the National Policy Council, an adjustment which though not essential would be most desirable for effective collaboration between the Legislative and Executive branches. Congress might become amenable in the long run if the NPC functioned well in practice; but, at the outset the objective should be to persuade Congress that, regardless of misgivings, the experiment is worth a fair trial.

Another objection is likely to be the ponderosity of the National Policy Council, with its proliferating panels, staffs, and research groups—a potential monstrosity quite capable of spawning committees, procedures, regulations, and red tape in such number and quantity as to bring the Executive branch to a standstill. To some it would suggest a perverted faith in organization and procedures for solving the complex problems of mankind without adequate consideration for the quality of the people who must inject ideas, vitality, and humanity into the government process.

All of these concerns have some validity and deserve a thoughtful answer. Any organizational device such as the NPC could be diverted from a useful to a harmful purpose if evil or unfit men were allowed to control and exploit it for their purposes. However, if the NPC performed its intended role of a senior deliberative forum for the formulation of national policy, advocates of all shades of opinion would have their day in court before the President in company with all other interested parties. Rarely have senior officials had such an opportunity in the past. As Army Chief of Staff, I never heard the arguments for domestic or economic programs although they were competing for national resources against the military programs I espoused. Exposure of spokesmen of rival causes to the views of their competitors should tend to dull the sharp edge of uninformed partisanship and bring greater rationality into the determination of national priorities. If, in practice, it were clear that the NPC was a fair tribunal—it would be the business of the President to see that justice is done—many of the forebodings would promptly disappear.

I see no reason to expect the NPC to increase immoderately the effective power of the President. It does not add to his responsibilities or to the power presently at his disposition or reduce the restraints placed upon him by the War Powers Act or by legislation limiting his freedom of action in the civil field. Contingent power remains contingent until Congress sees fit to facilitate Presidential access to it. In a period of better feeling between the White House and Congress, I would hope that the requirement for the President to get specific congressional authority to use any economic weapon against a foreign opponent could be moderated. It should be possible at least to give him standby authority to take certain actions subject to specific congressional approval before carrying them out. Such authority could reduce the time now required to debate not merely the principle but also the ways and means of using nonmilitary weapons in the national interest.

As to the expanded dimensions that the National Policy Council may assume, I do not view elephantiasis as an inevitable development. While there is substance to Parkinson's Law of bureaucratic proliferation, the latter can be restrained by determined supervision. We are proposing no new functions for the Executive branch beyond those now being performed or attempted under adverse conditions. Our hope is merely to assure better performance under circumstances favoring better planning, programming, and supervision. In short, we are trying to reduce loss of Executive power due to internal friction, leaky valves, and ill-trained engineers—not to take power away from the Legislative, the Judicial, or the people and give it to the President.

So we are not advocating bigger government, but better government. But there may be an objection even to this course. I sometimes encounter views to the effect that, since any government is necessarily a danger to popular liberties, good or efficient government may be a greater danger since it will be more difficult to resist if oppressive or to overthrow if violence becomes necessary. Since Mr. Nixon, by abusing his Presidential powers, demonstrated the reality of this danger, let us reduce, not increase, Presidential strength. Since an arrogant White House staff once ran amok, let us henceforth curtail the White House personnel and organization supporting future Presidents. To preserve our liberties from big government, let us transfer power to local government and thereby circumvent the venal panderers to special interests now infesting the federal halls of government. So this thesis seems to run.

While a weakening of the Presidency may recommend itself to some, such an attitude ignores the realities of national growth and the impossibility of shunting wide-ranging problems like inflation and recession—no less than interstate commerce and the postal service —to a local level for resolution. Such problems require highly trained officials surveying from a national vantage point the activities of the economic-social sectors with the same unremitting attention as those who concentrate on foreign-military dangers. Planned inefficiency is an indulgence we cannot afford in this conflict-prone world. Oddly, it is often those who most loudly assail the "Washington mess" and deplore the size and derogate the competence of the federal government who make the heaviest demands on it for social services, guaranteed income, public health, and federal intervention in support of favorite causes.

Meanwhile, our spoiled, affluent nation, accustomed to unlimited resources, is running out of means to pay for the waste, luxuries, and follies inherent in our past way of life. We have no real choices as between big or little government—by the nature of the problems, it must be big in its capabilities and, in addition, as efficient as the human mind, character, and ingenuity can make it.

For me, the most troublesome question about the National Policy Council is whether it would be capable of attracting the kind of people necessary to man it. Somehow we must find ways to make government service appealing to our most promising young men and women, instilling in them a willingness to dedicate their careers to this indispensable work. Over time, the military services have been reasonably successful in this respect. Even in the lean years, when pay was meager and promotion slow, most of my generation in the Army somehow acquired a lasting vocation for the military service derived from family background, historical studies, the influence of a West Point education, or early associations with congenial service comrades. How to instill a similar feeling in the civil servants of government is our task today.

In England, Oxford and Cambridge have always produced outstanding political leaders, diplomats, and government administrators. In France, the Grandes Écoles have turned out many of the career officials needed to serve a highly centralized government. In the United States, there has been too little public esteem for government service to attract the best of the university crop and there are no government institutions specialized in training selected undergraduates and instilling in them a vocation for public service after the manner of the service academies. We need to do something analogous to perform this function for the civil sector.

Elsewhere I have suggested advanced training for a limited group of civil officials in a Center for Policy Research. This could be useful, but it does not meet the problem of attracting numbers of promising young people early in life. For the latter, the government departments should emulate the techniques of big business in proselyting talent on the campuses and offering inducements to bring graduates into government service. The inducements could include postgraduate training in the universities leading to advanced degrees in return for an agreement to serve for a certain minimum period. A longer-range possibility would be the creation of an Institute for Government Management offering both undergraduate and graduate courses for selected students. The successful graduates of the Institute, as well as those trained in the Center for Policy Research, could be formed into an Executive Corps with the pay, career patterns, and retirement privileges comparable to those of the Foreign Service and of the officer corps in the Department of Defense.

But for these devices to have any permanent success, there must be a change in popular outlook toward government service. It must enjoy the esteem bestowed on military service in time of war without the neglect into which it falls in postwar periods. Whether we like it or not, Washington is the principal scene of decisive national action and participation in government, the sure way to play a significant part.

IX

Can We Remain Secure?

The overall purpose of this book has been to develop in outline a national security policy consistent with the changes to be expected in the nature of security during the next decade. In so doing, I have sought to take into account the increasing number of valuables requiring protection and the likely threats to which they may be exposed. Of necessity, I have been obliged to advance many personal judgments on controversial matters such as the relative probability of various forms of war, the major objectives of future foreign policy, the proper size of the military budget, and the kind of armed forces that should be maintained. Now it would be only fair to ask whether I believe that such a security policy, if put into effect, would indeed assure our security in the period ahead.

My answer to such a question would be a cautious affirmative, subject to two restrictive provisos. The first of these is that the subsidiary decisions taken in implementing the policy and designing the supporting programs would be generally consistent with the scope and requirements of national security as set forth in the preceding chapters. There are many such decisions to be taken which would affect the outcome of the policy.

As merely the outline of a policy, there is necessarily much unfinished business in the proposal in its abbreviated form. Prior to final approval, Executive and congressional authorities would have to reach a consensus on many points about which thus far only my personal views have been offered—such things as the valuables requiring protection, the dangers justifying counterpreparations, and the resources to be set aside for security purposes. Final determinations about such matters would have to take into account the views of the voters who would eventually pass judgment on the validity of the national interests involved and would punish policy makers who had miscalculated the popular will.

The security policy I have advocated could be rendered inadequate by imprudent decisions or commitments of foreign policy that outran the capability of security forces to support them or that imposed excessive tasks on these forces, thereby curtailing their ability to provide protection elsewhere to other national interests. An example of a goal of foreign policy exceeding national capabilities is found in the broad language of the Truman Doctrine of 1947 pledging U.S. resistance to Communist aggression virtually any place any time. A more recent example of handicapping our security forces was the action of Congress in halting military aid to Turkey in 1975, thereby alienating a vital ally and restricting American effectiveness in restoring and maintaining peace in the Mideast.

Decisions in the military field could have a similarly adverse effect on the outcome of security policy. If our leaders decided to embark on a numbers race with the Soviets in strategic weapons, the result would be to waste resources badly needed elsewhere for more constructive purposes. Even if they chose to downgrade the importance of numbers and settle for strategic forces able to destroy the Soviet Union Z times, their ultimate wisdom would depend on the value they assigned to Z.

The effectiveness of conventional forces will depend on the readiness and mobility of a strong reaction force in the central reserve at home, one which is relatively independent of partially trained Reserve forces. Overreliance on the Reserves would impose delay on effective military reaction or result in sending forces of unequal readiness into action overseas. An early decision by policy makers on this matter would be needed in order to guide mobilization planning and to allow timely notification to allies affected by the decision.

The Navy would need answers to a series of questions regarding its future missions and responsibilities. Since it can never patrol every sparkling wave of blue water, it should receive priority guidance for keeping sea lanes open in peacetime and in specific war situations. It should know how far to plan on nuclear propulsion for its new ships. If there is serious thought of eliminating land-based ICBMs and transferring their missions to navy submarines, that decision is already overdue. If the amphibious mission of the Marine Corps is in danger of curtailment, action should be taken to redefine its tasks. Decisions on such questions, if made without an overview of all security needs, could distort the general pattern and result in excesses and deficiencies in the allocation of resources.

Perhaps the most critical decision affecting the military component would be that regarding the authorized personnel strength and the size of the overall military budget. I have advocated acceptance of a personnel authorization of 2.1 million volunteers (the uniformed strength in 1975) and a normal budget representing about 8 per cent of the GNP. I have no strong defense for that particular percentage or the linkage to the GNP, but it is important for the country to accept the need to pay a substantial annual premium for security that is roughly related to the increasing value of our assets and possessions to be protected. It is also important to change the congressional scrutiny of the budget from a line-item approach to a broad survey of the capabilities of our forces to do the principal tasks that we expect from them.

Budget formulation is made simpler today by the fact that the armed forces can hardly afford financially more men on their payrolls than they now have. Hence the key question facing government policy makers becomes: How much money above the fixed charges for training and maintaining a force of 2.1 million will be required for new equipment, research and development, and the accumulation of war reserves to assure the desired capabilities of the armed forces? The aggregated dollar requirement for both fixed and variable costs under anticipated conditions would, I believe, be in the neighborhood of 8 per cent of the GNP; but it is the method, not the figure, that is fundamentally important. In any case, in the wake of our defeat in Vietnam, I would hope that Congress would be inclined to give generous support to the armed forces. We shall need them not only to perform their usual tasks but also to make an increased contribution as strength-in-being to a restoration of our standing and authority in world affairs.

In outlining the proposed national security policy, we remarked on the need to review our alliances and commitments to see if they are still valid. If this point is accepted, the White House and the State Department would be obliged to make specific determinations as to which commitments are definitely outmoded and what new alignments, if any, should replace them. What specific nations will be able to help us in dealing with global problems like population growth, hunger, and nuclear proliferation? Which ones have economic assets capable of complementing our deficiencies? How can we remove obsolete commitments from the books without offending the cosignatories or alarming allies whom we wish to retain? Some degree of success in getting greater help from alliances is an essential part of our national security policy.

In trying to reinforce the civil component, I have proposed the National Policy Council in its general form and with a broad statement of purpose but with limited structural details. If the concept received official favor, much additional work would be necessary to fill in the interstices, particularly those in the organization and tasks of the Council panels and the Center for Policy Research. Many questions remain unanswered regarding the use of the Council in integrating multiple forms of power in support of national policy. How would it mesh its activities with the internal organization of Congress? How can the power of the President be held within proper bounds if he is given prearranged grants of authority to deal with sudden military crises and to respond effectively to foreign acts of economic warfare? If the Council were established, what elements of the Executive branch could be abolished and their functions transferred to this new creation? The way these specific issues were decided would exercise a determinative influence on the success or failure of the security policy we have recommended.

From this tabulation of open questions and issues requiring decision one can see the need for my proviso that all such matters must be settled consistently and positively if the overall policy is to assure our security. While this proviso constitutes a substantial protective qualification to my "cautious affirmative," I have felt obliged to propose still another—the necessity for prolonged survival to correct our self-destructive practices and tendencies.

In the foregoing chapters, many examples have been cited of internal weaknesses and tendencies which sap our strength and diminish the resources available to assure our security. Some have been individual traits of character; others are collective attitudes and predelections; not a few suggest a general aimlessness of national purpose, a weariness of spirit, a sterile skepticism, and an exaggerated distrust of conventional virtue worthy of the effete Romans described by Gibbon. His words on the difficulties of raising military manpower in the terminal period of the Empire recall our own resort to highly paid volunteers to man the armed forces:

> The timid and luxurious inhabitants of a declining empire must be allured into the [military] service by the hopes of profit or the dread of punishment. The resources of the Roman treasury were exhausted by the increase in pay, by the repetition of donatives and by the invention of new emoluments.

While I would not suggest that the United States is in the condition of fifth-century Rome, there are ample signs and symptoms in our ways of life that have often in the past been associated with decadence.

While decay is not necessarily a form of self-destruction, we have other proclivities that clearly are—wastefulness, for example. We Americans are notoriously profligate of our health, wealth, time, and talents. We are sinfully wasteful of food, energy, and natural resources. We consume far more than our per-capita share of the world's raw materials, displaying a selfish extravagance which outrages the less fortunate countries of the world, fans anti-American sentiment among them, and augments demands for a world-wide redistribution of wealth.

Thrift is not the only antique virtue that has lost its votaries. Rising generations seem to have repudiated many of the traits of character that we have admired in our forebears and thought we possessed—self-reliance, the "work ethic," love of country, and respect for parents, law, and authority. Citizens no longer rush to assist a victim of crime or to give testimony against lawbreakers. It often appears that the injunctions of the Ten Commandments against murder, adultery, theft, lying, covetousness, blasphemy, and filial impiety are considered no longer operative. The pledged word has lost its sanctity—the abandonment of our Vietnam ally on the battlefield hardly raised a cry of outrage from the public, seemingly indifferent or unaware of its significance.

While there is no dearth of critics of government and the "Washington mess," there are few volunteers for public service among our best-qualified citizens. As a result, we have often delivered government—and with it our security and well-being—into the hands of mediocrities and time servers. While we are probably getting the government we deserve, it is not of a quality offering much hope of overcoming the complex problems ahead.

Although the Founding Fathers, Madison in particular, gave us repeated warnings of the dangers arising from factions, their modern versions abound in the form of minorities aligned on the basis of race, color, national origin, economic status, or sex. Many have become permanent centers of political power capable of exercising pressure at any point in the political apparatus.

If one accepts Plato's definition of justice as being a condition in which everyone attends to his own business and keeps out of his neighbors', injustice is rife in American public life. The Executive makes *de facto* treaties by executive agreement in order to bypass the Senate and in effect legislates the behavior of business and industry through its regulatory agencies. No longer content with declaring war, Congress now establishes the conditions for waging it and is prepared to modify by ex post facto legislation military commitments established by treaty. The courts legislate through interpretations of the law and from time to time take over the administrative functions of local school boards in prescribing ways and means to accomplish desegregation. In the summer of 1975, maritime unions undertook to decide national policy on grain sales to the Soviets.

In private life one finds similar examples of Platonic injustice. Liberated women wish to replace men everywhere but on the battlefield; but men, unfortunately, make no reciprocal offer to take over the homes—which go untended. In such a climate the cobbler regularly ignores his last and the country remains without the programs needed for economic viability and national security.

Among the self-destructive forces in the nation, one must accord a high place to those elements of the media that use their opinion-formative power to confuse, mislead, or bias the views of a public dependent on them for reliable news about the world and its contents. The mass communications at their disposition are so powerful, persistent, and pervasive that their continuing drumfire can unsettle and eventually benumb the judgment of the toughest, most sophisticated minds. If its masters use this power to provide the public with reliable information and clarifying interpretations regarding current events, if they openly take sides in public issues and explain the reasons for their preference, if they criticize government mercilessly but fairly when criticism is due, they are performing the indispensable functions of a free press in a democracy and justifying the constitutional privileges accorded it.

Unhappily such conduct is not always typical of media. Historically, there is a strong tendency among them to view the newsworthy as consisting largely of the sensational, abnormal, or criminal happenings of the world and to stress the ambient evil which threatens to engulf us. Such selective reporting may become a kind of censorship, screening out the wholesome and inspiring aspects of American life and creating a false impression of its quality. To the extent that this practice contributes to widespread suspicion, distrust, and doubts about ourselves and our institutions, it is a self-destructive practice encouraging a conviction that the United States contains little worth living or dying for.

Partisan political attitudes toward a President and his policies may result in a different kind of selective reporting which stresses points in support of editorial positions but excludes items unfavorable or adverse to them. By concentrating for years on the negative factors in the Vietnam situation (of which there were many), determined antiwar reporters succeeded in convincing a large part of the American public that South Vietnam and its people either could not be saved or were not worth our effort to save them. This conviction contributed to the disastrous finale of American policy in the spring of 1975 with consequences to national security previously discussed.

Even in performing the historic task of a free press in protecting the people against governmental oppression, an exaggerated zeal may commit excesses adverse to the public interest. If in exposing corruption and folly in government, the impression is made that all or most of our officials are rascals or fools, it will hardly contribute to attracting to Washington the talents for which we have a pressing need. While there have always been undesirables and incompetents in government, the vast majority of officials whom I have known in the course of half a century have been honorable, hard-working men and women who earn their pay—a thought that rarely breaks through the selective reporting of press and television. The price paid for denigrating public service is high—a general reluctance to work for the government, distrust of its officials and procedures, and a general feeling of alienation from government and absence of responsibility for it.

Can we expect the fulfillment of the two provisos which I have cited as necessary conditions to the success of our security policy? In some cases the difficulties should not be too great. It should be possible to reach agreement as to the valuables requiring protection, the dangers justifying countermeasures, and, in general terms, the resources that should be available for security purposes. There should not be too much trouble in gaining approval for a military component designed on the proposed lines and for a broad review of our principal alliances and commitments.

If these assumptions are correct, we would have satisfied the conditions of the first proviso except for the strengthening of the nonmilitary component. On this latter point I am not optimistic. I would expect the authorities responsible for approval of my suggestions to be lukewarm toward measures for readiness to wage economic warfare in time of peace, and many would resist the changes in the Executive status quo implicit in the concept of the National Policy Council.

The proviso that we must learn to curb our suicidal propensities would raise even greater difficulties. Many of our self-destructive traits are too deeply ingrained to permit easy eradication. But some things we certainly can do. We can raise the performance of government by means of organizational improvements and the devices proposed earlier to make public service more attractive to able young men and women. Incentives can be found to restrain wasteful habits and needless consumption. We might even find ways to persuade Congress to reduce the time expended on titillating investigations of marginal value and return to the dull but essential tasks of timely lawmaking. However, we are a nation of busybodies who will never completely forego the pleasure of trespassing on the greener pastures of other people's business.

We have other shortcomings which will be difficult to control. No way is likely to be found to moderate the growth of minority factionalism to the detriment of national interests, of which security is a primary one. Most minority groupings are bound together by a common urge to change the status quo, usually through a redistribution of wealth in their own favor. The propagation and perpetuation of these alignments are encouraged by the pliability of officials and politicians to their pressures—indeed, many public men pride themselves on being their spokesmen. Under such conditions, we can expect pressure groups to flourish, multiply, and continue to wield political power often in ways inimical to the general interest.

Another disabling characteristic of our system is the unwillingness of politicians to risk the political consequences of imposing unpopular measures on the electorate even to forestall clearly impending dangers. A salient example has been the reluctance of Congress, even after the OPEC oil embargo, to take decisive action to curb oil consumption and move toward independence from foreign oil suppliers. Any such action would be sure to produce unpleasant effects in raising the price of oil, requiring higher taxes, or both, and hence would be abhorrent to elected officials. As a result, three years after a clear recognition of the danger, the country remains without an energy program.

I have mentioned the ways in which the media may confuse and mislead public opinion and, by emphasizing the negative factors in our civilization, undermine our faith and confidence in the American system. For the sake of our security and well-being, I would hope for some moderation of these destructive tendencies on the part of an institution so vital to our democratic system. However, the tendency to shy away from prickly issues is likely to deter remedial action by Congress or the Executive. Meanwhile, there has been no synchronized effort on the part of media leaders to take action on their own initiative.

It is just possible that public opinion might force government and media to seek some amicable accommodation, perhaps in the form of a concordat setting forth guidelines of behavior for Executive and media representatives. Both sides have cause for mutual recrimination—the officials over antigovernment bias and violations of official privacy; the media over efforts to withhold or "manage" the news, lack of official candor, and the excessive security classification of government documents. Under the circumstances, there might be a common interest in developing a two-sided code of conduct—but that is, I fear, a remote hope.

A final, disturbing phenomenon difficult to curb is the rivalry for primacy and prestige, which of late has characterized relations between the President and Congress. While partially the result of opposite party control of the two branches, the present adversary relationship reflects other causes for hostility growing out of the highhanded treatment often accorded Congress in the Johnson and Nixon administrations. Under a Constitution that provides for no senior authority short of the Supreme Court to settle intestine disputes, feuding within and between branches of the government contains an ever-present danger of stalemate or at least interminable delay in the conduct of the most serious business of government. National security is in deep trouble unless we can restore the spirit of cooperation between the parts of government which is essential to its effective functioning.

From the foregoing survey of intractable self-destructive propensities, I feel bound to conclude that while our national security policy is well worth trying, there is no clear assurance that we can remain secure either under it or any other security policy. Although our country enjoys unusual assets in a sound political system, a flexible and resilient economy, reliable, nonpolitical armed forces, and a certain basic common sense which in the long run usually regulates the national behavior, our security is precarious as it enters the last quarter of the century.

It is worth repeating that in this coming period, we shall be confronted by formidable enemies both abroad and at home. Our most important foreign opponent seems likely to remain the Soviet Union, which continues to rearm at a rate and to a degree seemingly unrelated to the needs of deterrence or self-defense. Moscow propagandists openly enjoy the sorry state of political and economic affairs in the West, which promises, they believe, the advent of new power relationships precedent to the ultimate triumph of world socialism and the collapse of capitalism. Despite lip service to *détente*, the Soviet leaders, paraphrasing Cato, never cease to proclaim that America must be destroyed—albeit, preferably from within.

Along the global south flank of the industrial world extends a loose coalition of some eighty have-not countries which are uniting to demand retroactive compensation for past wrongs and present privations. The United States is the prime target of their resentment, symbolizing to them the affluence, selfishness, and voracity of the have-world responsible for their backwardness. If voiced, their slogan would be: "America must be despoiled."

We have a third front at home where the danger arises from a miscellany of groups composed in large part of frustrated, alienated, misguided, or revolutionary people who, finding no good in American leaders, institutions, motives, or accomplishments, see no hope for improvement without radical change. In contributing to disunity, disillusionment, and unrest, these groups also appear dedicated to the downfall of America by undermining its strength and reinforcing self-destructive tendencies already at work within our society.

Oddly, we received due warning of this danger more than a century ago from Lord Macaulay, the English historian, who, in a letter in 1857 to an American friend discussing the future of our country, uttered a prediction highly relevant to our theme:

> The United States will be fearfully plundered and laid waste by barbarians in the twentieth century as the Roman Empire was in the fifth—but with this difference. Your Huns and Vandals will have been engendered within your own country by your own institutions.

Macaulay based his prediction on an expectation that, in our democracy, the poor majority among its citizens would eventually rise to despoil the rich, thereby destroying our civilization or causing the rise of a dictatorship to restore order. While he did not anticipate the stabilizing influence of a strong, well-to-do middle class such as later arose in America and the effectiveness of our tax system in transferring wealth in support of social programs, his warning against dangers from within is well worth heeding, particularly at a time when we have potential despoilers beyond our walls as well as within. But the latter are the more dangerous by their closeness to the vitals of state and society.

This grim view of the precariousness of our situation is not without patches of sunlight. Many of the weaknesses we perceive within ourselves have their counterparts in foreign nations. The USSR has its quota of troubles—hostile frontiers, inability to feed an increasingly restive people, and a serious succession problem arising upon the eventual departure of Brezhnev from the political scene. A signal difference between our two nations is the constant striving by the Soviets, only partially successful, to conceal their weaknesses and protect their image of power from loss of awe, while Americans delight in letting all their dirty linen "hang out" and inviting in the neighbors to look at it.

The have-not world is still deeply divided and remains handicapped by the absence of leadership, capital, and adequate food for their exploding populations. The danger that they represent to world peace and order is rising but has not yet approached its crest.

Thus, urgent measures are required if we are to control the Vandals and self-destructive forces within. This can be done, I feel sure, if we have the will to submit ourselves to a stern program of regeneration, to reject decadent ways, and to seek out new and dynamic causes to serve as goals for a purposeful life.

One such cause could be national security and the efforts of its forces to defend our valuables from harm. The changes that are occurring in its scope and nature will affect the lives of all of us, who, as citizens, will share the consequences of change and hence must concert in forestalling those adverse to our security.

Thus, we must regard ourselves as participants in a contest for survival, not as bystanders observing a struggle that we can entrust to the security forces of government. We are players on the field, not spectators in the grandstand; we are among the gladiators and the lions of the Coliseum, not judges in the upper boxes turning thumbs up or down on the protagonists in the arena. This is our struggle for security and the outcome rests largely on us. We should have learned by experience that government cannot give us happiness—at most, only the opportunity to pursue it. National security is a similarly elusive goal and its achievement is equally beyond the gift of government and dependent on the character and quality of the people who would enjoy it.

Index